BLM

A Review of
BLACK-FOOTED FERRET
Reintroduction
in Northwest Colorado, 2001–2006

Technical Note 426
August 2008

Prepared by:

Brian E. Holmes
Wildlife Biologist
Bureau of Land Management
White River Field Office
220 East Market Street
Meeker, Colorado 81641

ACKNOWLEDGMENTS

THE REINTRODUCTION of black-footed ferrets in Colorado has been made possible by the dedicated work of many individuals from a variety of agencies and organizations. In particular, Mike Albee of the Bureau of Land Management in Craig, Colorado, and Bob Leachman of the U.S. Fish and Wildlife Service in Grand Junction, Colorado, had the vision and laid the groundwork upon which all subsequent work has been based. In addition, the following people or groups have contributed greatly to the recovery of black-footed ferrets in Colorado and, in many cases, elsewhere:

Desa Ausmus
Lisa Belmonte
Brent Bibles
Dean Biggins
Gene Byrne
Cross Mountain Ranch
Mike Grode
Ed Hollowed
Mike Lockhart
Al Pfister

Beverly Rave
Lonnie Renner
Pam Schnurr
Dale Skidmore
Stacey Smith
Scott Winkler
Wolf Creek Work Group
Lisa Wolfe
Terry Wygant
Bart Zwetzig

CONTENTS

LIST OF ILLUSTRATIONS

FIGURES

ABSTRACT

BETWEEN THE FALL OF 2001 and the end of 2006, 217 black-footed ferrets *(Mustela nigripes)* were released within the Wolf Creek Management Area (WCMA) in northwest Colorado in an effort to reestablish this species within its former range. Following 5 years of releases and monitoring, the minimum prebreeding (spring) population within the WCMA in 2006 was 9 ferrets and the minimum population at the end of 2006 was 13 ferrets. While survival of released captive-raised ferrets was high for some colonies in the eastern portion of the WCMA, survival throughout much of the rest of the area was low compared to other ferret reintroduction sites. Three wild-born kits from three separate litters were documented, representing a major step in the recovery effort. However, the observed average litter size of 1.0 was also lower than other reintroduction sites and is probably insufficient to maintain the population without yearly supplemental releases. Overall minimum ferret population size in the WCMA increased steadily from 2002 to 2006, as did the population of their primary prey, the white-tailed prairie dog *(Cynomys leucurus)*. Observed differences in ferret survival and numbers of wild-born kits produced in different portions of the WCMA appear to be driven primarily by differences in habitat quality (the density of prairie dogs and their burrows). This reintroduction program has contributed valuable information for research and management needs pertinent to ferret recovery rangewide, and work continues toward the establishment of a viable population and recovery of this species in Colorado.

INTRODUCTION

BLACK-FOOTED FERRETS *(Mustela nigripes)* are listed as "endangered" under the Endangered Species Act (ESA) and historically occurred throughout the grasslands and intermountain basins of west-central North America where populations of prairie dogs *(Cynomys spp.)* occurred. Once thought extinct, a remnant population of ferrets was found near Meeteetse, Wyoming, in 1981, but this population subsequently declined, and the last remaining animals were captured to begin a captive-breeding program in 1987. Since then, ferrets have been reintroduced within their historical range at sites in six of the United States (Arizona, Colorado, Montana, South Dakota, Utah, and Wyoming) and in the State of Chihuahua, Mexico. No additional wild populations have been discovered to date. A thorough review of the background and history of the black-footed ferret recovery program can be found in Lockhart et al. (2006).

Black-footed ferrets are specialist predators of prairie dogs and historically occurred throughout Colorado in association with colonies of black-tailed (*C. ludovicianus*), white-tailed (*C. leucurus*), and Gunnison's (*C. gunnisoni*) prairie dogs (figure 1). However, populations declined and the ferret was eventually eliminated from its range in Colorado coincident with prairie dog eradication efforts, conversion of native prairie to other land uses, and disease outbreaks in the first half of the 20th century. The last confirmed ferret sighting in northwest Colorado occurred near Craig in Moffat County in 1943, and the last confirmed ferret sighting in the State occurred in Costilla County in 1946 (Anderson et al. 1986).

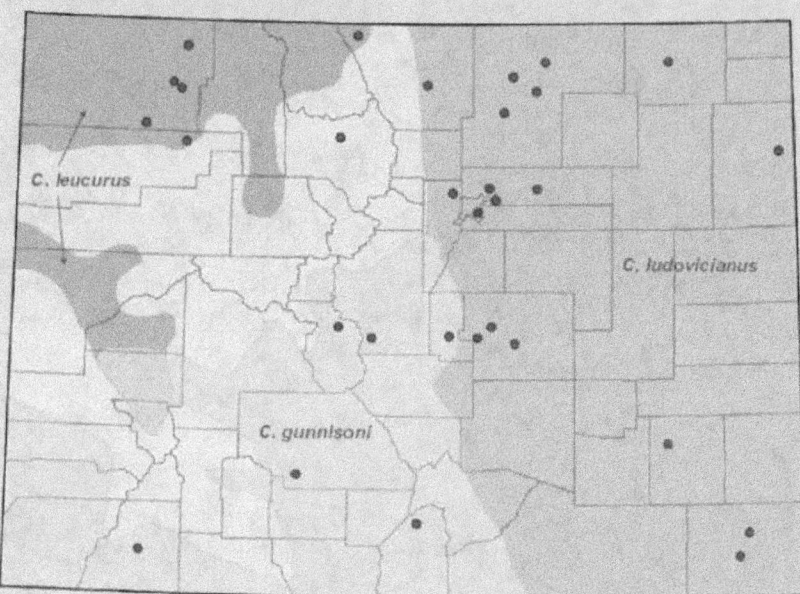

Figure 1. Historic distribution records of black-footed ferrets and the range of three prairie dog species in Colorado (after Anderson et al. 1986).

This report summarizes black-footed ferret reintroduction and recovery activities conducted within the Wolf Creek Management Area in northwest Colorado from 2001 through 2006. Reintroduction of black-footed ferrets in Colorado began in 2001 with the release of captive-bred ferrets into the Wolf Creek Management Area and Coyote Basin Management Area (figure 2).

The primary purpose of this reintroduction is to establish a self-sustaining population of ferrets in the wild in Colorado as part of a wider effort to restore populations of this species within its former range. Another goal of the program is to accomplish ferret recovery in northwest Colorado in a manner that is consistent with existing local lifestyles and economies. While a portion

of the Coyote Basin site does occur in Colorado, it is managed as part of the ferret recovery program in Utah and will not be addressed in this report.

Cooperating Agencies and Parties

The recovery program for black-footed ferrets in northwest Colorado is a cooperative effort among the Colorado Division of Wildlife (CDOW), Utah Division of Wildlife Resources (UDWR), Bureau of Land Management (BLM), U.S. Fish and Wildlife Service (USFWS), and U.S. Geological Survey–Biological Resources Division (USGS–BRD). Because of the geographic location of reintroduction sites and proximity of ferret recovery efforts in Colorado and Utah, these two programs are closely linked, and many aspects of ferret recovery planning in the two States are coordinated by a single group, the Colorado/Utah Black-Footed Ferret Working Group. This group consists of representatives from those

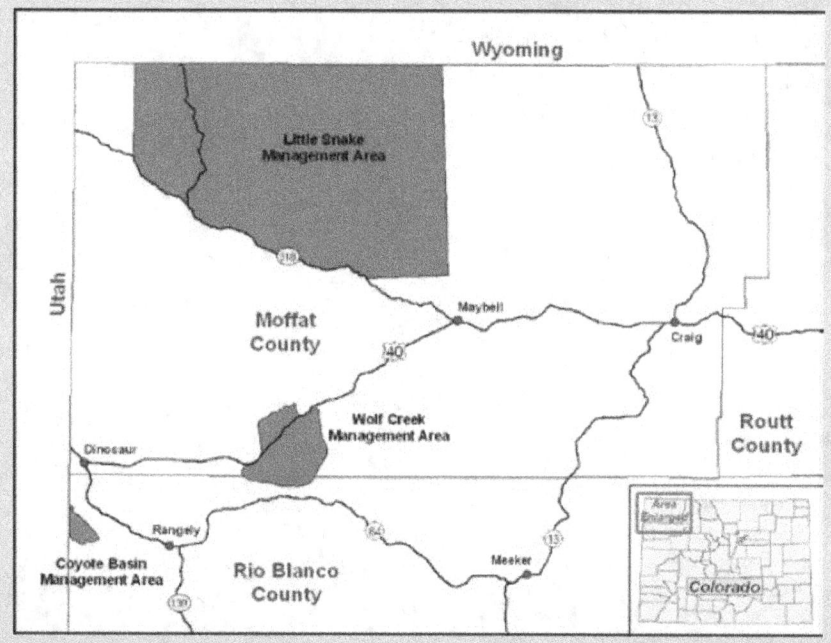

Figure 2. Location of the three black-footed ferret management areas in northwest Colorado.

agencies listed above including three BLM field offices: the White River Field Office in Meeker, Colorado; the Little Snake Field Office in Craig, Colorado; and the Vernal Field Office in Vernal, Utah. In addition to these agencies, support for the program also comes from the Uintah Basin Campus of Utah State University (USU) and from the Animal and Plant Health Inspection Service (APHIS)—Wildlife Services. USU personnel provide technical advice and support for a variety of issues, including ferret management and monitoring, prairie dog monitoring, and disease research, while APHIS assists in collecting biological samples for implementation of the disease monitoring protocol associated with ferret reintroduction.

Program History and Authorization

Shortly after the remnant population of black-footed ferrets was found near Meeteetse, Wyoming, in 1981, CDOW and USFWS began searching for an existing population of ferrets in Colorado. At that time, they also began the process of identifying potential sites where ferrets could be reintroduced into Colorado in the future. While no ferrets were found during these efforts, three sites in northwest Colorado were identified as having potential for ferret reintroduction. These were the Little Snake Management Area in northwest Moffat County, the Wolf Creek Management Area in Moffat and Rio Blanco Counties, and the Coyote Basin Management Area in Rio Blanco County, which would be managed as part of a larger site in Coyote Basin, Utah. These areas were identified as suitable sites because each consisted of large complexes

of white-tailed prairie dog colonies that occurred primarily on public lands.

Once the final animals were captured from the Meeteetse, Wyoming, population in 1987 and captive breeding began, plans were immediately put in place to begin reintroducing ferrets into suitable habitat once the captive population was secure. The national Black-Footed Ferret Recovery Plan (U.S. Fish and Wildlife Service 1988) identified three recovery objectives:

1) Increase the captive population of black-footed ferrets to a census size of 200 breeding adults by 1991;

2) Establish a prebreeding census population of 1,500 free-ranging black-footed ferret breeding adults in 10 or more populations with no fewer than 30 breeding adults in any population by the year 2010; and

3) Encourage the widest possible distribution of reintroduced black-footed ferret populations.

Black-footed ferret reintroduction in northwest Colorado was authorized in 1998 with publication in the "Federal Register" of the final rule for "Endangered and Threatened Wildlife and Plants: Establishment of a Nonessential Experimental Population of Black-footed Ferrets in Northwestern Colorado and Northeastern Utah" (U.S. Fish and Wildlife Service 1998). Under section 10(j) of the ESA, as amended, the USFWS may designate reintroduced populations as experimental and nonessential to the continued existence of the species. This designation gives Federal agencies more flexibility in managing the species by relaxing the responsibilities in section 7

of the ESA. Section 7 directs all Federal agencies to use their authorities to conserve threatened and endangered species and ensure that their actions do not jeopardize listed species or destroy or adversely modify critical habitat. Populations designated as nonessential and experimental are treated as proposed for listing and are given fewer protections than a fully listed species. This designation also often increases local support for the reintroduction of listed species by giving assurances that current and future land uses will not be disrupted by the action. The experimental population area in northwest Colorado includes all of Moffat and Rio Blanco Counties west of State Highway 13.

The reintroduction of black-footed ferrets into Colorado also required State legislative approval. The Colorado State Legislature approved the reintroduction on April 18, 2000, through House Bill 1314. This legislation and the subsequent Colorado Revised Statute 33-2-105.6 required that ferret reintroduction activities be conducted in a manner consistent with the approach used in the management plan for the Little Snake Management Area (U.S. Fish and Wildlife Service et al. 1995). Additionally, it called for recovery cooperators to provide regular updates to the local community on the status of reintroduction activities and required that representatives of local government and affected interests be involved in the resolution of issues that may arise during the reintroduction effort.

The original area planned for ferret releases in Colorado was the Little Snake Management Area. In 1989, this area contained at least 31,720 hectares (78,400 acres) of active white-tailed prairie dog colonies, with approximately 95 percent of this occupied habitat occurring on BLM-administered public lands. However, this population of prairie dogs declined throughout the late 1990s, presumably due to an outbreak of sylvatic plague. As a result, the site was removed from consideration for ferret releases and another site was sought. The Wolf Creek Management Area (WCMA), located approximately 30 km (19 mi) south of the Little Snake Management Area, continued to support a sizeable white-tailed prairie dog population during this period and was identified as a suitable alternative release site.

In February 2000, the Wolf Creek Work Group was formed in order to develop a consensus-based management plan that would serve as a steering document for ferret recovery in the Wolf Creek and Coyote Basin (Colorado) Management Areas. This group consisted of representatives from BLM, CDOW, county government, recreational groups, energy companies, and the public at large. The product of the group's work was "A Cooperative Plan for Black-Footed Ferret Reintroduction and Management— Wolf Creek and Coyote Basin Management Areas, Moffat and Rio Blanco Counties, Colorado" (Wolf Creek Work Group 2001). This plan was patterned after a similar plan for the Little Snake Management Area in northwest Moffat County (U.S. Fish and Wildlife Service et al. 1995) and addressed all aspects of ferret management, including physical, biological, and social resources within the management areas; management roles associated with ferret recovery; program goals and objectives; land use issues and management strategies; and anticipated activities associated with implementation of the plan. A primary goal identified in the plan was that ferret recovery would be conducted in a way that was compatible with existing and future economies and lifestyles, including live-stock management, mineral development, and recreation activities. The plan also called for ferret recovery in Wolf Creek to be a cooperative effort among Federal, State, and local governments and private entities.

METHODS

Description of the Wolf Creek Management Area

THE WOLF CREEK MANAGEMENT AREA (WCMA) is located in northwest Colorado in Moffat and Rio Blanco counties (figure 3). Land ownership within the management area is predominantly public, BLM-administered land (90 percent) under the jurisdiction of the BLM's White River Field Office. The remainder of the area consists of State (6 percent) and private (4 percent) holdings. The WCMA encompasses a large basin of approximately 21,000 hectares (52,000 acres) at the lower reaches of the Wolf Creek watershed; Wolf Creek is a tributary of the White River. The WCMA is

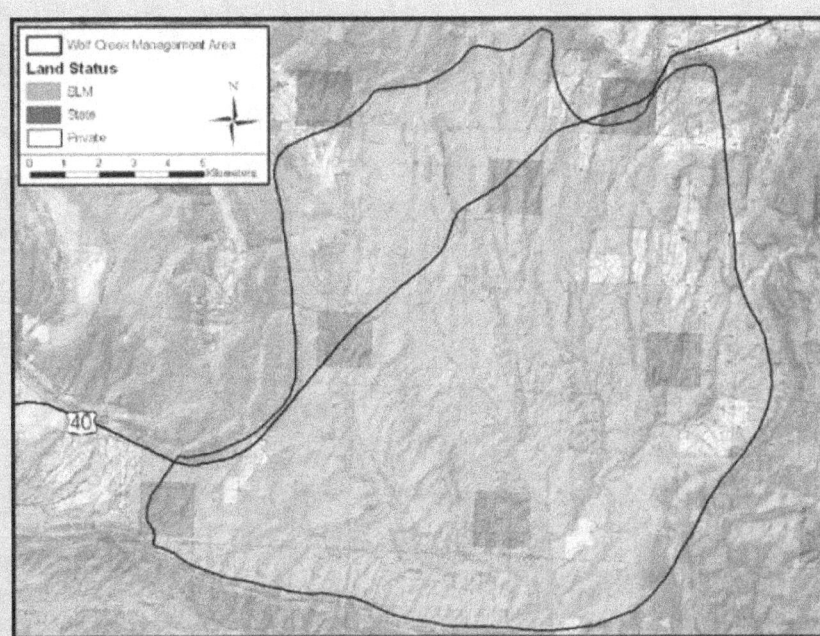

Figure 3. Land ownership within the Wolf Creek Management Area.

bounded on the south by Coal Ridge, on the east by Pinyon Ridge, and on the north by Elk Springs Ridge and its associated uplands stretching westward. The western end of the basin is contiguous with habitat occupied by prairie dogs that stretches without major geographic barriers all the way to the Colorado/Utah State line; however, the western boundary of the management area was defined as Moffat County Road 95C because the proportion of privately held land increases substantially west of that point. Elevations range from 1,665 to 1,890 meters (5,460 to 6,200 feet), and the topography is characterized by rolling hills and sloping valleys dissected by deeply cut drainages. Along the borders of the basin, there are typically steep escarpments that define the transition to surrounding uplands. The climate is continental and arid, characterized by cold winters and hot summers. Average yearly precipitation at the two nearest recording stations at Rangely, Colorado, about 25 km (16 mi) southwest of the WCMA, and Dinosaur, Colorado, about 30 km (19 mi) west of the WCMA), is 25.45 cm (10.02 in) and 29.57 cm (11.64 in), respectively (Western Regional Climate Center 2007).

The major plant community present within the WCMA is the salt-desert shrub association, which is dominated by several shrub species and characterized by a sparse herbaceous understory. Common shrubs in these habitats include big sagebrush *(Artemisia tridentata)*, black greasewood *(Sarcobatus vermiculatus)*, winterfat *(Krascheninnikovia lanata)*, and several species of saltbushes *(Atriplex* spp.*)*. Understory species include western wheatgrass *(Pascopyrum smithii)*, Salina wildrye *(Leymus salina)*, Sandberg bluegrass *(Poa secunda)*, cheatgrass *(Bromus tectorum)*, and a variety of annual and perennial

forbs. Along the eastern margin of the management area, there are more pure stands of big sagebrush as well as several large drainage bottoms dominated by grasslands. In addition to the grass- and shrub-dominated communities present, there are also several stands of pinyon-juniper *(Pinus edulis-Juniperus osteosperma)* woodland present on ridgetops and where elevations are higher within the WCMA. Pinyon-juniper woodland is also the dominant habitat type surrounding the basin. Riparian habitat types are extremely limited within the WCMA, as even the main stem of Wolf Creek is intermittent. The little riparian habitat that exists is typically associated with artificial water impoundments.

The primary land uses within the WCMA are livestock grazing and big game hunting. Livestock grazing consists of winter sheep use and winter/spring cattle use. In general, the northern and eastern portions of the WCMA consist of sheep allotments, while the southern and western portions consist of cattle allotments. Slight reductions in

overall grazing duration and intensity were incorporated into grazing permits reissued for several allotments within the WCMA since 2001. These reductions were intended to improve range condition and might be expected to improve the forage base available to native herbivores, including prairie dogs. Big game hunting for pronghorn antelope *(Antilocapra americana)*, mule deer *(Odocoileus hemionus)*, and elk *(Cervus elaphus)* occurs throughout the WCMA. Hunting activity generally occurs from August to October for pronghorn and during November and December for deer and elk.

Prairie Dog Management and Monitoring

There were approximately 7,700 hectares (19,000 acres) of active white-tailed prairie dog colonies distributed throughout the WCMA in 2006 (figures 4 and 5), although that figure certainly fluctuates on an annual

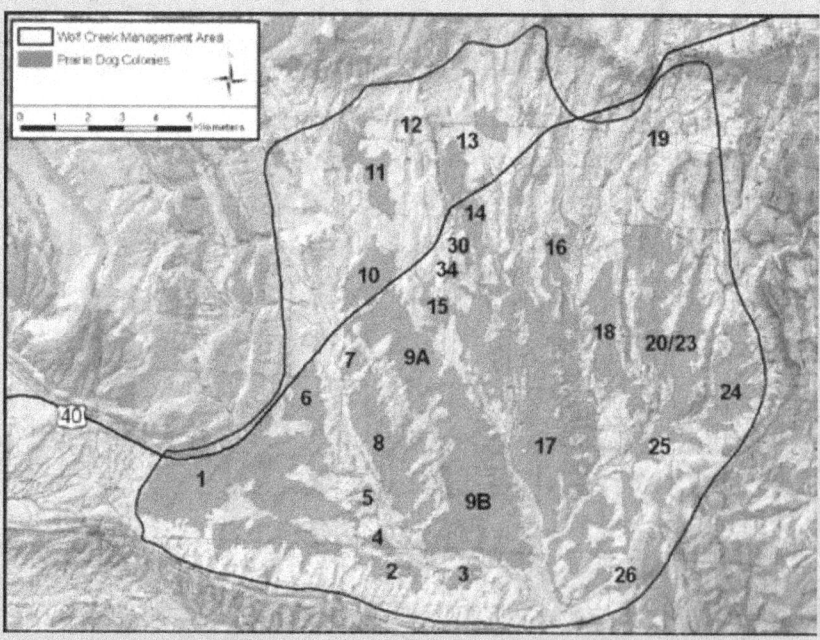

Figure 4. White-tailed prairie dog distribution within the Wolf Creek Management Area. Colonies are labeled with numbers referred to in the text and in Appendix A.

Figure 5. An example of white-tailed prairie dog and black-footed ferret habitat within the Wolf Creek Management Area. This is a photograph of part of colony 20/23, where ferrets were found routinely during 2005 and 2006. Pinyon Ridge, the eastern boundary of the Wolf Creek Management Area, is in the background.

basis. Total occupied acreage was estimated at 6,800 ha (16,800 ac) in 2001 when black-footed ferrets were first released. Colony sizes in 2006 ranged from 11 ha (27 ac) to 1,460 ha (3,608 ac).

Land management activities within the WCMA that are administered by the BLM are conducted with the objective of maintaining at least 6,270 ha (15,500 ac) of occupied white-tailed prairie dog habitat (Wolf Creek Work Group 2001). Surface-disturbing activities are permitted with conditions to avoid prairie dog colonies where possible, and offsite habitat enhancement for the purpose of increasing occupied prairie dog acreage is the preferred method of mitigation where adverse impacts to prairie dog colonies within the WCMA are unavoidable. Much of the WCMA

was leased for oil and gas development in May 2006, but no exploration or development activities had occurred on these leases as of the end of 2006.

No special prairie dog shooting management guidelines were established in the WCMA as a result of black-footed ferret reintroduction because the perceived level of harvest in the area was assumed to be compatible with ferret habitat objectives. As such, management of prairie dogs in the WCMA remained consistent with statewide regulations. White-tailed prairie dogs in Colorado were historically managed as a small game species with a year-round season of harvest and unlimited bag and possession limits. However, in September 2006, the Colorado Wildlife Commission passed a regulation that limited the season

of harvest of all three species of prairie dogs in Colorado to June 15 through February 28 to limit take during the period when prairie dogs are reproducing and have dependent young. This seasonal closure took effect in 2007 and applies only to public lands (both Federal and State).

For the purpose of identifying complexes of prairie dog colonies suitable as black-footed ferret habitat, Biggins et al. (1993) proposed a method by which a group of colonies that are each within 7 km (4.4 mi) of one another are considered a complex and among which ferret movements may be expected. Demographically, such a complex would be expected to support a population of ferrets that exchanged individuals and genetic material among colonies. The 7-km distance was based on the longest observed nightly movement of a ferret in the remnant Meeteetse population. However, Biggins et al. (2006a) proposed modifying the 7-km distance to a distance of 1.5 km (.9 mi) based on observed movements of reintroduced ferrets at UL Bend National Wildlife Refuge in Montana, where 85.5 percent of all intercolony movements were <1.5 km (Biggins et al. 2006b). This 1.5-km distance is now accepted as a more typical intercolony or dispersal movement distance and is currently used to circumscribe complexes of prairie dog colonies for the purpose of ferret reintroduction.

In addition to defining a complex and determining total acreage occupied by prairie dogs, Biggins et al. (1993) also identified prairie dog abundance as a critical component of evaluating potential ferret habitat. They proposed a method by which belt transects 1,000 m (3,281 ft) long and 3 m (10 ft) wide are used to quantify prairie dog burrow density. Along these transects, the total number of active and inactive burrows are quantified. Active burrow density can then be used to estimate prairie dog population density and abundance and, based on ferret energetics, determine a minimum number of ferrets that a complex can support. This number is called the ferret family rating (FFR) where one "ferret family" consists of an adult female, her litter, and one-half of an adult male ferret. The minimum density of prairie dogs required to support a female ferret raising a litter based on this model was 3.63 prairie dogs/ha, and areas supporting this minimum density of prairie dogs were considered "good habitat."

Based on the modified 1.5-km complex circumspection rule, all colonies in the WCMA were considered to represent one complex. The transecting method to determine prairie dog density and the minimum

number of ferrets that an area should support was employed in the WCMA beginning in 1989. However, different areas within the WCMA, sampling intensity, and sampling frequency were used throughout that time to quantify prairie dog population characteristics. Methods and transect routes were finally standardized in 2004. Table 1 reports summary statistics for 5 years of transecting data. Data from 2002 and 2003 are comparable to one another but not to data from 2004 to 2006 due to variations in methodology. Colony-specific transect summaries for 2004 to 2006 are included as Appendix A.

Wide fluctuations in prairie dog density, abundance, and FFR, such as those observed in the WCMA, are probably common in white-tailed prairie dog populations. These fluctuations are likely due to climatic factors and disease or some combination of these factors. The observed increase in prairie dog abundance in the WCMA from 2004 to 2006 was most likely due to a return to average or above-average precipitation during 2005 and 2006 following the drought years of 2002 and 2003 (Western Regional Climate Center 2007). Both Maxfield (undated) and Van Pelt and Winstead (2003) indicated that prairie dog populations in their study areas appeared to fluctuate in response to climatic factors.

Disease Management and Monitoring

Two diseases, sylvatic plague and canine distemper virus (CDV), have played a prominent role in the management and

conservation of black-footed ferrets throughout their range. Sylvatic plague is a flea-borne zoonotic disease (one that is maintained in wildlife populations but transferable to humans) caused by the bacterium *Yersinia pestis* that was introduced into North America from Asia around 1900. It is highly virulent to all species of prairie dogs and has been indicated as one of the primary threats to the persistence of prairie dog populations and recovery of the black-footed ferret throughout North America (Barnes 1993, Cully and Williams 2001). In addition to causing high mortality within their primary prey, *Y. pestis* is also highly virulent to ferrets (Williams et al. 1994). CDV is a viral pathogen commonly spread by aerosol that causes central nervous system disease in infected animals. This disease primarily affects carnivores, although other taxa can also be affected. Black-footed ferrets are highly susceptible to CDV, which they are probably most often exposed to through interactions or habitat overlap with wild and unvaccinated domestic canids (Williams et al. 1988). Both sylvatic plague and CDV were found present at the Meeteetse, Wyoming, site in 1985 during a decline in the ferret population there, and these diseases probably acted synergistically in causing that decline, which eventually led to the elimination of black-footed ferrets in the wild.

Table 1. White-tailed prairie dog population attributes within the Wolf Creek Management Area, 2002 to 2006.

Year	Prairie Dog/Ha — Entire Complex	Population Estimate — Entire Complex	% Good Habitat	Prairie Dog/Ha - Good Habitat	Population Estimate — Good Habitat	FFR
2002	3.2	18,843	38	6.6	14,846	18.4
2003	3.4	19,968	41	6.8	16,564	21.9
2004	2.7	21,112	29	7.0	15,485	19.6
2005	4.3	33,309	50	6.9	27,615	36.1
2006	7.2	52,650	74	9.1	49,519	64.1

To monitor the status of select diseases that may compromise the suitability of the WCMA as ferret habitat, coyotes *(Canis latrans)* were tested for serological evidence of exposure to *Y. pestis* and CDV within the WCMA each year from 2000 to 2005. In addition, coyotes were also tested for serological evidence of exposure to tularemia, a disease caused by the bacterium *Francisella tularensis*, which is not known to adversely affect ferrets but can cause mortality in rodents and lagomorphs. Serological surveys for disease determine exposure by looking for the presence of pathogen-specific antibodies in the blood of a host. A positive result indicates only that the host was exposed to the pathogen sometime during its life. The collection of coyotes was accomplished in cooperation with CDOW and APHIS–Wildlife Services. Coyotes were collected through a combination of calling and aerial gunning. Targeted sample sizes each year were 20, while actual sample size ranged from 11 to 21.

Evidence of exposure to *Y. pestis* among coyotes in the WCMA was absent each year from 2000 to 2003, but increased slightly each year in 2004 and 2005 (table 2). However, this increase in plague seroprevalence, or the rate at which blood serum from coyotes tested positive for plague, during those years did not appear to indicate an active plague outbreak because prairie dog populations also increased during that time period. Seroprevalence of exposure to CDV varied by year, but was generally low. The highest number of CDV seropositive coyotes (those with CDV antibodies present in the blood) were collected in 2000 (19 percent of those sampled were positive) and 2001 (28 percent were positive), but these results indicate that this pathogen is probably consistently present within the WCMA. In contrast to plague and CDV, tularemia

seroprevalence was high each year of sampling, with the proportion of positive coyotes ranging from 26 percent to 44 percent. As with plague, though, the presence of tularemia did not appear to have a great negative effect on prairie dog populations, as they have increased in the presence of seemingly high tularemia infection rates.

Because of cost and some limitations inherent in interpreting the results of disease surveillance conducted through opportunistic carnivore sampling, this method was discontinued in 2006. As an alternative, disease surveillance was accomplished through sampling small mammals within the WCMA. This method offers greater spatial and temporal resolution in monitoring disease activity due to the small home ranges and short lifespans typical of most small mammals. A much larger sample size was gathered using this method, and it was also more economical than contracting through APHIS–Wildlife Services. Staff from the CDOW Wildlife Health Program managed the sampling, which consisted of taking blood samples from live-trapped small mammals at a number of locations within the WCMA. Samples were tested for evidence of exposure to plague and tularemia but not CDV because rodents are not known to be hosts for CDV. Field sampling was carried out in early August 2006 and samples were gathered from 303 small mammals representing the following genera: *Peromyscus* (n=290), *Tamias* (n=10), *Onychomys* (n=2), and

Reithrodontomys (n=1). All samples were negative for plague and tularemia.

Two prairie dog colonies totaling 347 ha (857 ac) were treated with an insecticide dust to kill fleas and reduce *Y. pestis* transmission during the summers of 2004 and 2005. This test was part of a collaborative research project to determine the efficacy of this treatment for increasing ferret and prairie dog survival. The goal was to identify whether low levels of *Y. pestis* infection may have been negatively impacting ferret or prairie dog survival. On the treated colonies (colonies 6 and 13) every burrow was treated with 4 g of 0.05 percent deltamethrin formulation (Delta Dust®, manufactured by Bayer

Table 2. Disease surveillance results from coyote serological surveys for the Wolf Creek Management Area, 2000 to 2005.

Sampling Period	Plague			
	# Tested	Positive	Negative	% Positive
2000	19	0	19	0.00
2001	17	0	17	0.00
2002	13	0	13	0.00
2003	11	0	11	0.00
2004	20	1	19	5.00
2005	19	4	15	21.05
	Canine Distemper Virus (CDV)			
	# Tested	Positive	Negative	% Positive
2000	21	4	17	19.05
2001	18	5	13	27.78
2002	12	0	12	0.00
2003	11	1	10	9.09
2004	20	1	19	5.00
2005	19	2	17	10.53
	Tularemia			
	# Tested	Positive	Negative	% Positive
2000	21	9	12	42.86
2001	16	7	9	43.75
2002	13	5	8	38.46
2003	11	3	8	27.27
2004	20	8	12	40.00
2005	19	5	14	26.32

Environmental Science, Montvale, New Jersey), a synthetic pyrethroid insecticide labeled for the control of fleas in rodent burrows. Subsequent ferret releases on these treatment colonies included both plague-vaccinated and control animals (see the "Releases" section). Treatment effects on ferret survival could not be determined because none of the ferrets released on these colonies during 2004 and 2005 were ever relocated. There was no apparent treatment effect on prairie dog populations at the two treatment colonies, based on yearly monitoring transects, but this method is probably not sensitive enough to detect small changes in survival. Furthermore, any treatment effect (or lack of treatment effect) could have been confounded by other factors including predation, recreational shooting pressure, or local habitat conditions, for which no controls were established.

Black-Footed Ferret Management

Allocation and Preconditioning

To obtain black-footed ferrets for release into the wild, agencies and organizations involved in ferret reintroduction submit allocation proposals to the USFWS. Sites requesting ferrets are ranked according to a number of factors, including suitability of habitat, disease status and management, past ferret survival, kit production, research contributions, and long-term site conservation. The final decision as to how many ferrets each site receives, as well as the sex and age makeup of those animals, is made by the USFWS's black-footed ferret recovery coordinator. The majority of ferrets released each year are captive-reared

animals that are produced at the National Black-Footed Ferret Conservation Center in Fort Collins, Colorado (formerly in Sybille, Wyoming). However, a number of other facilities also have captive-breeding programs for black-footed ferrets and contribute to the pool of ferrets available each year for release into the wild. In addition, some wild-born ferrets from the Conata Basin reintroduction site in South Dakota have been captured and transplanted to other sites.

Captive-bred ferrets reared in cages and released into the wild with no prerelease experience living in a natural environment or capturing live prey have lower survival rates than animals preconditioned in quasi-natural environments (Biggins et al. 1998). Because of this, ferret preconditioning has been an integral part of the Colorado reintroduction program. The BLM's Little Snake Field Office manages "onsite" preconditioning pens near Browns Park in Moffat County. The site was built on a white-tailed prairie dog colony and consists of 20 pens, each about 21 by 21 meters (70 by 70 feet). White-tailed prairie dogs are trapped by CDOW each year from near Grand Junction, Colorado, and provided to the facility for preconditioning activities. Ferrets allocated to both Colorado and Utah were maintained in these pens for 30 to 60 days, during which time they were exposed to the natural environment of prairie dog burrows and to live prairie dogs so that they could develop hunting skills.

Releases

A total of 217 ferrets were released in the WCMA from 2001 to 2006 (table 3, figure 6). Of those, 184 (85 percent) were kits when they were released and 33 (15 percent) were adults. The release of captive-born ferrets occurs in the late summer or fall to correspond with the time period when kits would naturally disperse from their maternal territory, so kits are the preferred age-class for release. Most ferrets (207/217, or 95 percent) released in the WCMA during this period were captive-raised animals that came from one of several facilities across the United States. However, 10 ferrets released in 2003 were wild-born animals that were transplanted from Conata Basin, South Dakota. The number of ferrets released in any given year ranged from 19 to 63. Appendix B details the origin and release data for all ferrets released within the WCMA. Appendix B also includes maps of release locations within the WCMA for all years but 2001, for which this data was not available.

Table 3. Summary of black-footed ferrets released within the Wolf Creek Management Area, 2001 to 2006.

Year	Sex	# Captive-Born Released		# Wild-Born Released	Total	Inclusive Release Dates	Year Total
		Kits	Adults	All Kits			
2001	Male	17	0	0	17	11/15/01 to 11/23/01	35
	Female	11	7	0	18		
2002	Male	8	1	0	9	8/15/02 to 11/19/02	28
	Female	12	7	0	19		
2003	Male	17	2	6	25	8/16/03 to 11/19/03	63
	Female	20	14	4	38		
2004	Male	25	0	0	25	10/6/04 to 11/16/04	44
	Female	18	1	0	19		
2005	Male	13	0	0	13	10/13/05 to 11/2/05	19
	Female	6	0	0	6		
2006	Male	17	0	0	17	9/26/06 to 11/9/06	28
	Female	10	1	0	11		
Grand Total							217

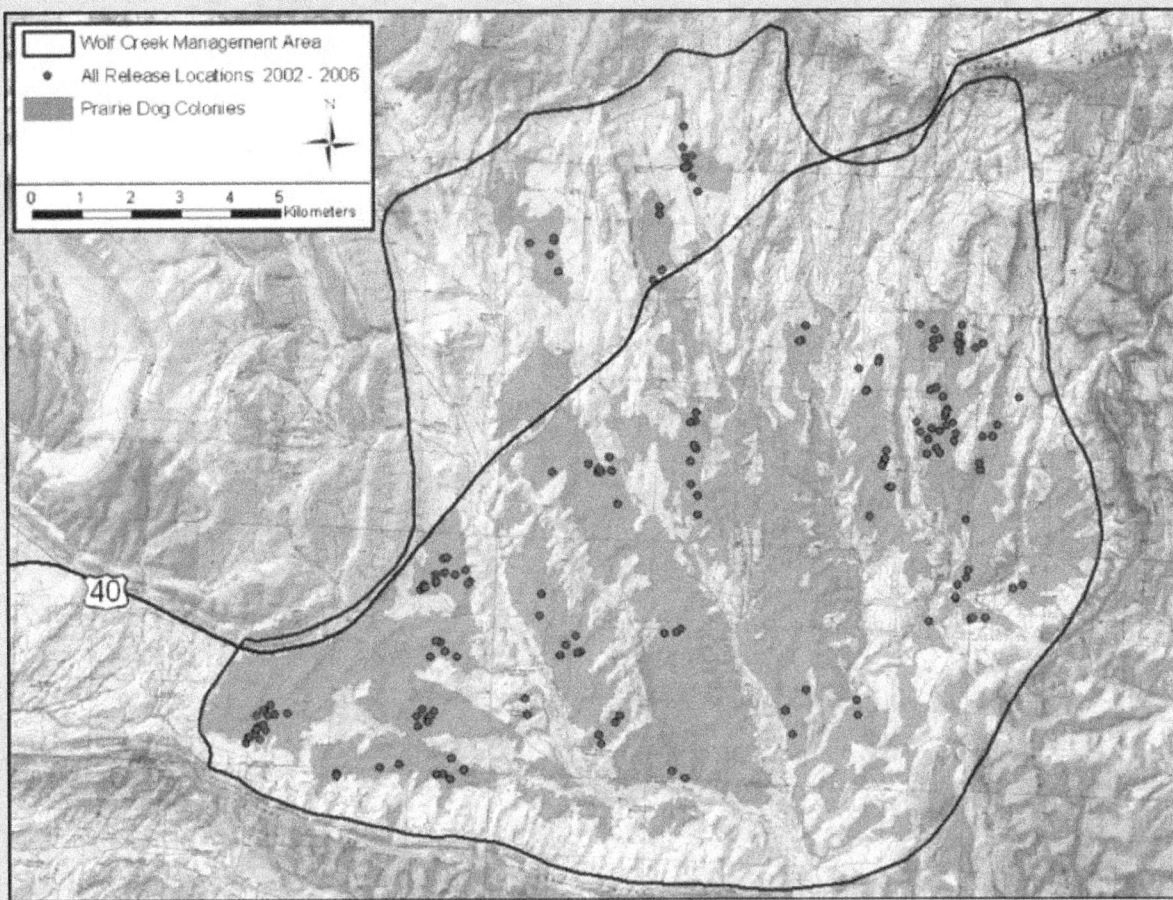

Figure 6. All black-footed ferret release locations within the Wolf Creek Management Area, 2002 to 2006 (2001 data not available).

All ferret releases in Colorado have been "hard" releases. That is, ferrets did not have onsite cages or nest boxes that they could return to following release. Instead, ferrets were released into areas of high prairie dog density (as determined by transecting) without further support. Areas with high prairie dog density were chosen for release because prey density is considered the most important habitat characteristic for ferrets (Biggins et al. 2006b). Prior to release, all ferrets were implanted with two passive integrated transponder (PIT) chips (American Veterinary Identification Devices, Norco, California). These chips, which are approximately the size of a large grain of rice, were implanted subcutaneously in the neck and near the pelvis. Each chip contains a unique nine-digit number that is activated by a specialized reader and allows for the individual identification of ferrets for the life of the animal. Two chips were implanted to create a redundancy whereby if one chip fails, identification can still be made with the remaining chip.

All ferrets released in the WCMA received a series of two canine distemper vaccinations (Purevax® Ferret Distemper, manufactured by Merial, Inc, Athens, Georgia). Beginning in 2004, a subset of ferrets also received a plague vaccine as part of a research program to determine whether vaccinating ferrets against plague would protect them against low levels of plague activity and increase survival. Increased survival of plague-vaccinated ferrets has been observed on black-tailed prairie dog habitat in Montana (D. Biggins, personal communication) and researchers desired to expand this research to include ferret reintroduction sites within white-tailed prairie dog habitat.

RESULTS

Monitoring Efforts

Spotlighting

THE MOST COMMONLY USED METHOD of monitoring black-footed ferrets is nocturnal spotlighting (Clark et al. 1984, Campbell et al. 1985). This method involves using high-intensity spotlights, either mounted on a vehicle or carried on foot, at night. The goal of this survey technique is to locate ferrets when they are most active at night by illuminating their characteristic bright, emerald green eyeshine. While the eyeshine of other animals such as coyotes, badgers (*Taxidea taxus*), and pronghorn also reflects green, positive identification of ferrets can be made by close approach of the animal in question. When spotlighting, searchers typically use continuous illumination while slowly moving through a prairie dog colony,

constantly scanning from dusk until dawn for a minimum of 3 consecutive nights.

The most intense spotlight surveys for ferrets in the WCMA took place each year, beginning in 2002, in either August or September, when kits are often active aboveground in litter groups and litter size and maternity can be quantified. These intense survey efforts were timed to coincide with the full moon and were held over 10-day periods so that multiple colonies could be adequately surveyed. Due to the large area of white-tailed prairie dogs in the WCMA, about 7,700 ha (19,000 ac), only a portion of the area could

be surveyed. Those colonies or portions of colonies that were surveyed each year were chosen based on past ferret occupancy and high prairie dog density as determined by yearly monitoring transects. In addition to the intense late summer spotlight surveys, additional surveys were conducted in the WCMA in the late fall and early winter (October to December) to determine the short-term survival of recently released ferrets and in the spring (March to April) to determine overwinter survival and identify the potential breeding population. Once a ferret was located, an attempt was made to either identify the animal with a hand-held

PIT reader by placing its circular antenna over the occupied burrow (figures 7a and b) or by trapping, depending on survey objectives. Any wild-born ferrets encountered were captured, implanted with two PIT chips, and given a CDV vaccination, as described previously for captive-born ferrets that were released into the wild.

Spotlight surveys were initiated in the WCMA in 2002, and the total survey effort ranged from about 700 hours to over 1,200 hours per year (figure 8). The majority of this effort was conducted on foot because vehicle travel in the WCMA is restricted to existing roads, and a relatively small proportion of the overall prairie dog colony acreage is visible from roads. The total number of individual ferrets observed within the WCMA each year is reported in table 4. Only confirmed observations are reported in table 4. Confirmed observations were those observations in the field that were made at close range to be sure that the animal was a black-footed ferret or those observations that resulted in a PIT chip reading or capture. Unconfirmed observations of green eyeshine are not included in these totals. Postrelease observations include animals that were released in a given year and that survived at least 30 days following release. These observations were made during the late fall and early winter survey period and are a standard measure of short-term survival in ferret recovery programs (e.g., Biggins et al. 2006c).

Radio Telemetry

The initial black-footed ferret release in the WCMA occurred on November 15, 2001, and consisted of 23 kits and 7 adults. To track postrelease movements and survival, the 23 kits were fitted with radio transmitters with a frequency range of 164–165 MHz and an average expected battery life of 45 days. Monitoring consisted of both aerial telemetry (five night flights and two day flights) and ground telemetry carried out from November 14, 2001, to January 7, 2002. Inclement weather resulted in fewer telemetry flights than were originally planned. Transmitters and collars from 10 of the ferrets were recovered: two were confirmed to be dropped collars, four were from ferret mortalities, and four were inconclusive as to whether they

Figure 7. a) An example of the 6-inch-diameter circular antenna of a hand-held passive integrated transponder (PIT) reader over the entrance of a prairie dog burrow.

Figure 7. b) In this picture, the PIT reader is in a storage pouch and connected to a 12 V power source.

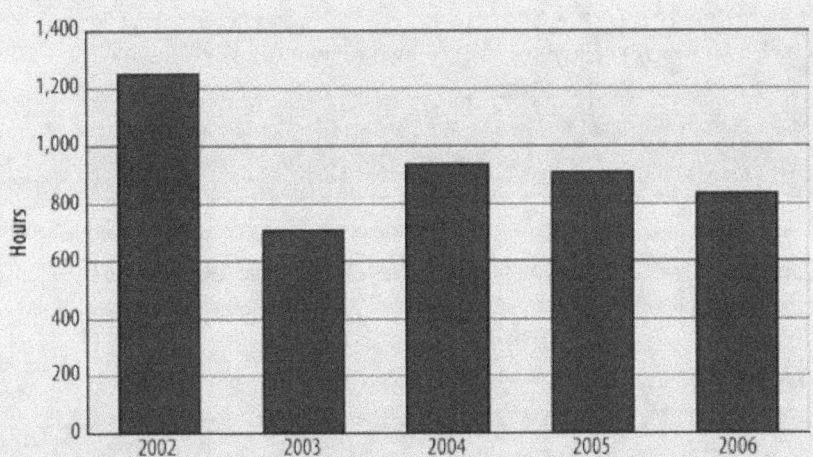

Figure 8. Total spotlighting survey effort by year in the Wolf Creek Management Area, 2002 to 2006. Bars represent total effort expended throughout the year, but the bulk of survey time occurred in August and September.

Table 4. Total number of individual black-footed ferrets observed within the Wolf Creek Management Area, 2001 to 2006.

	2001	2002	2003	2004	2005	2006
Ferrets Alive 30 Days Postrelease	6	1	2	3	6	3
Ferrets From Previous Years	N/A	1	1	3	6	8
Wild-Born Ferrets	N/A	0	0	0	1	2
Minimum Yearend Population Estimate	6	2	3	6	13	13

were dropped collars or mortalities. The four mortalities were determined to be caused by a coyote in two cases, a golden eagle *(Aquila chrysaetos)*, and an unknown raptor. Of the remaining 13 ferrets from which transmitters were not recovered, several were relocated during telemetry monitoring up to 3 weeks following their release, but many were not relocated again following release. A conservative estimate of short-term (30-day) mortality was 26 percent (6/23) for these first kits released in the WCMA.

In the fall of 2005, 11 captive-raised ferrets were again fitted with radio transmitters prior to release in an effort to document postrelease movements and survival. Spotlight surveys between 2002 and 2004 had resulted in very few ferret observations and

the telemetry work carried out during the fall and early winter of 2005 was intended to help address some questions regarding the short-term survival and movements of captive-raised ferrets released into the wild within the WCMA. The radio transmitters (Wildlife Materials, Inc., Murphysboro, Illinois) weighed approximately 5 g (.18 oz), had a 20-cm (7.9-inch) whip antenna, and were affixed to animals as described in Biggins et al. (2006c). The frequency range used was 150-151 MHz, and the transmitters had an average expected battery life of 50 days. Radio-collared animals were released between October 13 and October 26, 2005, and followed using hand-held receivers (model: R-1000; Communication Specialists, Inc., Orange, California) and three-element folding Yagi antennas.

Of the 11 animals released with radio collars, three were killed by predators within 1 week of release. The heads of two ferrets, with collars still attached, were

found shallowly buried outside of the colony where the ferrets were released, which was consistent with coyote predation observed during ferret telemetry work at other reintroduction sites (D. Biggins, personal communication). The third mortality was confirmed upon retrieval of the ferret's collar, which showed evidence of predation, including a rip and bite marks on the transmitter package; however, the type of predator could not be confirmed. Of the remaining eight radio-collared ferrets, six shed their collars within several days of their release, one was not located again beginning the day after its release, and one was followed for the life of the collar. Shed collars were confirmed by excavating the burrow within which the collar was stationary for more than 3 consecutive days. The single ferret that was followed for the life of its collar was a juvenile male released on October 19, 2005. This individual remained at the colony where he was released (colony 25) while moving about 750 m (2,461 ft) to the east during the telemetry monitoring period; he still occupied this same general area at the end of 2006 as determined by spotlight surveys.

Because a large proportion of radio-collared ferrets shed their collars shortly after release, data gained on postrelease movements and survival of captive-raised animals released in the WCMA were minimal. However, this telemetry work did confirm some trends seen at other release sites, namely that captive-raised ferrets can be particularly susceptible to predation shortly after release and that ferrets released into good habitat with sufficient prey may demonstrate limited postrelease movements, thereby increasing survival by limiting exposure to predators and reducing energetic expenditure.

Working Dogs for Conservation

Working Dogs for Conservation is an organization based in Three Forks, Montana, that specializes in using scent dogs to detect wildlife species and their signs. In May 2005, they were contracted to conduct searches for black-footed ferrets in the WCMA because spotlight searches conducted during the previous 3 years had resulted in few confirmed ferret detections. Two dogs trained to indicate on the scent of live ferrets, both with previous experience in ferret searches, searched for a total of approximately 37 hours on seven different colonies. Between the two dogs, a total of 36 burrows were indicated, suggesting ferret occupancy. Of those burrows indicated by one dog, four were "confirmed" by blind "double-checking" by the second dog, which indicated on the same burrow. In four other cases, the second dog indicated on a burrow within 50 m (164 ft) of a burrow indicated by the first dog. However, followup spotlight searches and PIT reader deployment on the eight "double-checked" burrows resulted in no confirmed ferret observations. Whitelaw et al. (2005) discuss interpretation of these results and offer further suggestions for the use of scent dogs in searches for black-footed ferrets.

Snowtracking

The use of snowtracking as a survey method for locating and studying black-footed ferrets was described by Clark et al. (1984). This technique was used opportunistically in the WCMA during the first 5 years of the reintroduction program when proper snow conditions existed. The locations of four individual ferrets were confirmed through snowtracking between December 2001 and February 2002, but no ferret locations have been confirmed through snowtracking since then. The snowtracking effort expended in the winter of 2001-2002 was 500 hours, but only about 80 hours of effort were expended each of the following two winters on snowtracking. Since then, only limited, opportunistic snowtracking efforts have been expended, mostly due to poor snow cover within the WCMA. However, given adequate snow conditions, snowtracking can be a useful tool in locating ferrets and studying winter movement patterns and habitat use (Richardson et al. 1987).

Reproduction in the Wild

The goal of the Wolf Creek black-footed ferret recovery program is to establish a self-sustaining population that does not require constant population augmentation. As such, reproduction by free-ranging ferrets is central to the success of the program. Three wild-born ferrets were documented within the WCMA by the end of 2006. The first wild-born kit was captured and marked on November 20, 2005, and two additional kits were captured and marked in September and November of 2006. While maternity was not confirmed for the kit (WC05-01) located in 2005, maternity was confirmed for the two kits (WC06-01, WC06-02) located in 2006. Ferret WC06-01 was the kit of WC05-01, the 1-year-old wild-born female from 2005, making her a second generation wild-born. Ferret WC06-02 was the kit of ferret 4884, a 1-year-old female released in 2005. All three wild-born kits came from colony 20/23 (a single large colony that is separated for the sake of prairie dog monitoring), and all three represented litters of one kit each.

Previously reported average litter sizes at emergence for ferrets in the wild include 3.5 (n=11) for ferrets inhabiting black-tailed prairie dog colonies in South Dakota (Linder et al. 1972, as reported in Hillman and Clark 1980), 2.2 (n=38) for reintroduced ferrets inhabiting black-tailed prairie dog colonies in Montana (Matchett 1999), and 3.3 (n=68) for ferrets inhabiting white-tailed prairie dog colonies at Meeteetse, Wyoming (Forrest et al. 1988). The average litter size of 1.0 observed in the WCMA was substantially lower than those reported values and is probably insufficient to compensate for annual mortality experienced at the site. Such small litter sizes may be a function of the energetic costs of females living in an environment with low prey densities. Overall prairie dog densities throughout the WCMA are the lowest reported from any current reintroduction site. Even though much of the area supported densities of at least 3.63 prairie dogs/ha, which Biggins et al. (1993) predicted to be the minimum density necessary to support reproducing females, reproduction was only documented in colonies with average prairie dog densities of greater than 5.5 prairie dogs/ha as determined by yearly transecting. In addition, females with litters appeared to use patches of high burrow densities within these colonies. This observation is consistent with recent work in South Dakota and Montana by Jachowski (2007), who found that female ferrets select and compete for patches of high prairie dog density on black-tailed prairie dog colonies in his study area, where prairie dog densities were much higher than those in the WCMA.

Population Size, Survival, and Movements

To date, black-footed ferret reintroduction programs have relied on spotlighting as the primary means of surveying for ferrets and determining population status. This tecnique, as presently used, only provides a minimum number of animals known to be alive. Therefore, a complete or near-complete survey of all habitat has been required to estimate minimum population size, and it is this figure that has been commonly used to report ferret population status.

The total number of ferrets observed each year is shown in table 4. The number of ferrets observed during 30-day postrelease surveys is an indicator of short-term survival of captive-born animals, but survey efforts during this time period (October–December) were not consistent from year to year. A better indicator of trends in the overall ferret population is the number of animals relocated from previous years and the number of wild-born ferrets detected during yearly summer surveys conducted in August or early September because efforts were similar each year. A steady increase in numbers was observed from 2002 to 2006, with a minimum yearend population of 13 ferrets in 2006.

A spring survey was conducted in the WCMA in mid-March of 2006. The purpose of this survey was to assess overwinter survival and document the minimum spring population size. A minimum prebreeding (spring) population of 30 ferrets was identified in the national recovery plan (U.S. Fish and Wildlife Service 1988) as a goal for individual reintroduction sites. Hours expended during this survey were much fewer than during the annual summer survey because of limited personnel; however, five ferrets were located with survey efforts concentrated on what was considered to be the best habitat. Subsequent surveys throughout 2006 found additional animals present that were not located during the spring survey, indicating that at least nine ferrets were present in the spring of 2006.

Figure 9 shows the locations of all black-footed ferrets observed from December 2001 until the end of 2006. The amount of search effort required per unique ferret

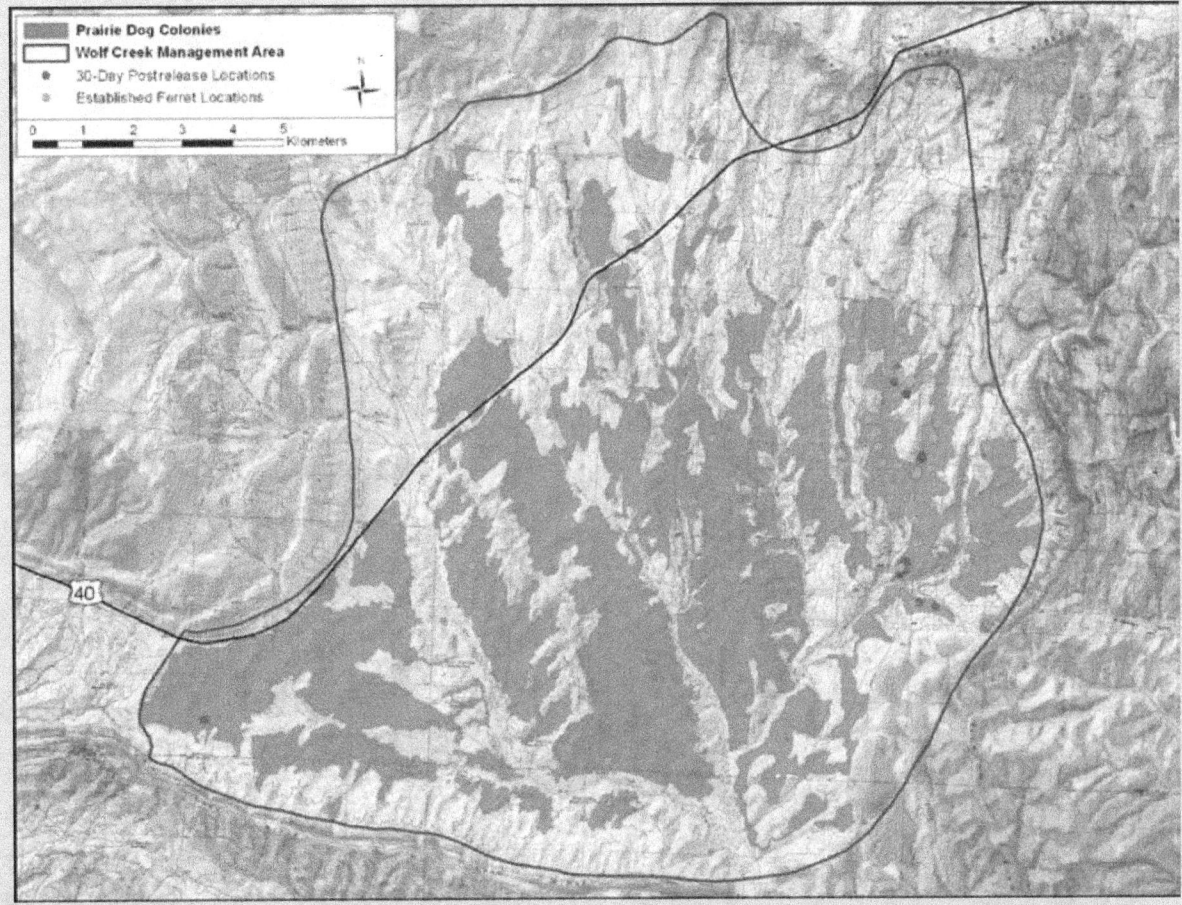

Figure 9. All black-footed ferret relocations within the Wolf Creek Management Area, 2001 to 2006. Locations in green represent 1) captive-born ferrets that survived to at least the following spring to enter their first breeding season and 2) wild-born ferrets. Locations in blue represent ferrets relocated in the year they were released that survived at least 30 days in the wild following release.

observation was 140 hours during the summer of 2005 (5 ferrets, 700 hours), 70 hours during the summer of 2006 (9 ferrets, 630 hours), and 18 hours during the spring of 2006 (5 ferrets, 90 hours), when only areas with the highest probability of containing ferrets were surveyed. These search effort figures are comparable to the amount of spotlighting time required per unique ferret observation at another reintroduction site on white-tailed prairie dog habitat in Shirley Basin, Wyoming, reported by Biggins et al. (2006d). There, search efforts ranged from 12 to 126 hours per unique observation with a median of 52 hours (n=8 survey periods).

Most of the ferrets observed to date have been located in the eastern portion of

the WCMA, and survival appears to differ among release colonies (see figure 6 vs. figure 9). The colonies in the eastern portion of the WCMA where most ferrets were located (colonies 18, 20/23, and 25) total about 1,100 ha (2,718 ac) in size and represent about 14 percent of the currently mapped prairie dog habitat in the WCMA. However, ferrets released in these colonies have been reencountered more often than ferrets released on other colonies in the WCMA. Too few ferrets were relocated from release cohorts prior to 2004 to make reliable estimates of survival; however, minimum apparent survival to 1 year for ferrets released in these eastern colonies was 33 percent (2/6) for ferrets released in 2004 and 43 percent (6/14) for ferrets released in 2005. In addition, all three

wild-born ferrets documented to date have come from these colonies. In contrast, minimum apparent survival to 1 year for ferrets released throughout the remainder of the WCMA colonies was 3 percent (1/38) for ferrets released in 2004 and 0 percent (0/5) for ferrets released in 2005. The one ferret from the 2004 release that was documented to have survived to 1 year, a female (4745), was relocated on colony 20/23 in the eastern portion of the WCMA the following summer, having dispersed more than 7 km (4.35 mi) from her release location (figure 10). This was the second ferret documented to disperse a long distance into colony 20/23; a male released in 2003 (P393) moved more than 10 km (6.21 mi) from his release location into this colony (crossing U.S. Highway 40 along the

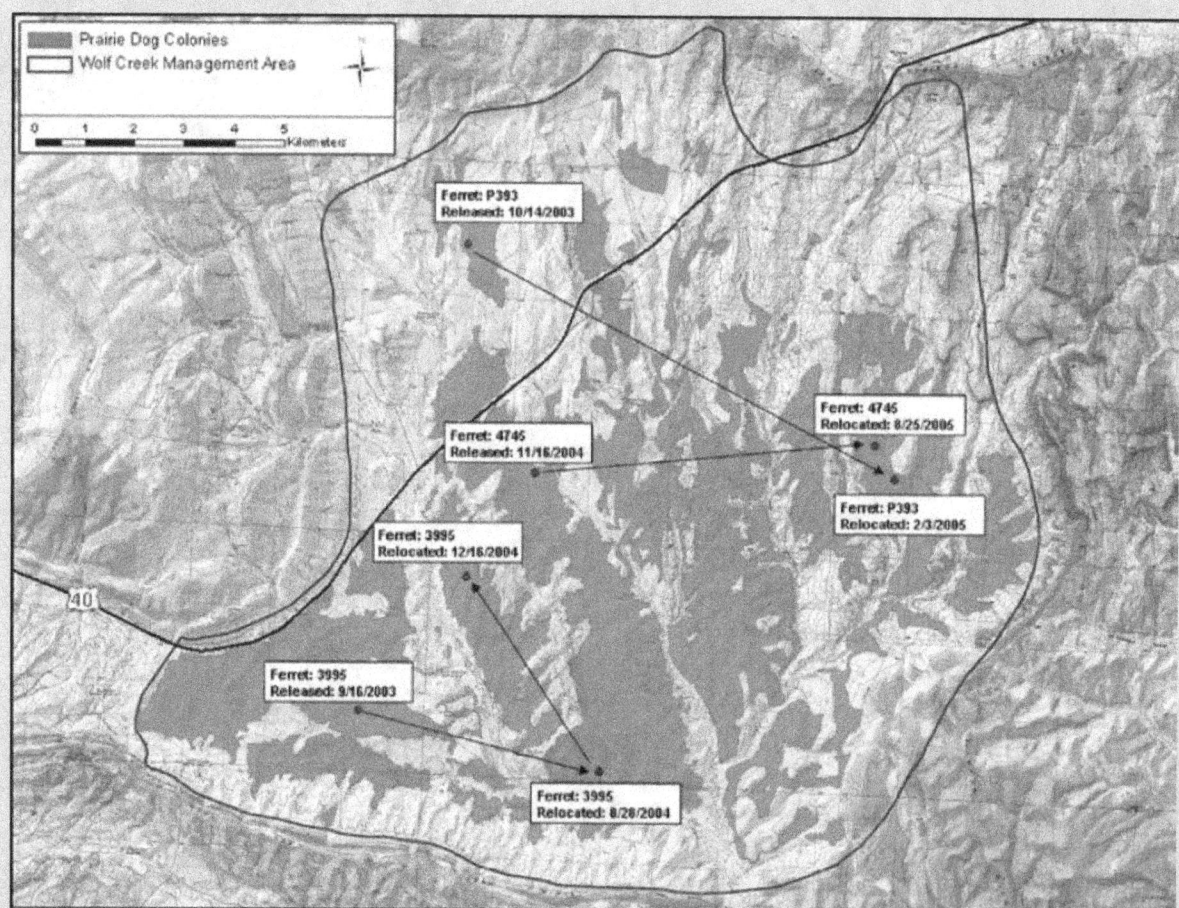

Figure 10. Documented long-distance, intercolony dispersal movements by ferrets within the Wolf Creek Management Area.

way), where he apparently established a territory and was relocated several more times. Ferret P393 was still alive at the end of 2006, making him 3.5 years old and one of the two oldest ferrets located to date in the WCMA. A female ferret (P316) was also documented to have survived to 3.5 years old when she was last located in December 2005.

Overall, long-term survival (survival to 1 year) for captive-raised ferrets released in the WCMA was low compared to other release sites, but survival of ferrets released on the three eastern colonies was equivalent to or higher than that recorded at other release sites (Biggins et al. 2006c). The observed differences in survival among colonies within the WCMA may have been due to differences in habitat quality, predation, disease dynamics, or other factors. In regard to habitat quality, prairie dog densities at colonies 18, 20/23, and

25 were consistently among the highest in the WCMA. In addition, the proportion of these colonies with a minimum density of 3.63 prairie dogs/ha, considered by Biggins et al. (1993) to represent "good" habitat, was also consistently high (Appendix A). In general, areas with high prairie dog density represent better habitat than areas with low prairie dog density because searching out and securing prey is less energetically costly. However, burrow density itself may also influence how ferrets use prairie dog colonies. Forrest et al. (1985) and Biggins et al. (2006b) discuss how areas with high burrow density would be beneficial to ferrets by providing escape cover and reducing the time spent aboveground traveling between burrows when ferrets are most susceptible to predators. Unfortunately, there is no data available on the abundance or distribution of potential ferret predators in the WCMA that might help explain observed differences in ferret survival.

Another factor possibly driving differences in ferret survival was disease, primarily plague. Beginning in 2004, approximately half of the ferrets released received a plague vaccine as part of an experimental trial to determine if this vaccine is effective in increasing ferret survival in areas where plague may exist at low levels. None of the three ferrets that were released in 2004 and relocated in summer 2005 had been vaccinated against plague, while four of the six ferrets released in 2005 and relocated in summer 2006 were vaccinated against plague. Results from this vaccine trial in the WCMA and in Coyote Basin, Utah, are equivocal so far, with no clear pattern of differences in survival between vaccinated and control groups.

DISCUSSION AND RECOMMENDATIONS

THE OBSERVED PATTERNS of ferret habitat use, survival, and reproduction in the wild imply that not all prairie dog colonies within the WCMA were equally suitable for ferrets, and in particular, for female ferrets attempting to raise a litter. Ferret survival and longevity within a subset of colonies in the eastern portion of the WCMA were equivalent to and, in some cases, higher than what has been observed at other reintroduction sites, including sites currently supporting large, apparently self-sustaining populations. However, survival in much of the rest of the WCMA was very low and all three litters documented were of a single surviving kit, which is also low compared to other reintroduction sites and probably insufficient to maintain a stable population in the absence of yearly supplemental releases.

The variable pattern of success observed at different colonies in the WCMA was probably not an artifact of survey procedures. While spotlighting is difficult within the WCMA because of rugged terrain, relatively heavy shrub cover, and lack of vehicle access, hundreds of hours of spotlighting were conducted each year, both within those colonies where survival and reproduction have been documented and in other colonies where few if any ferrets have been relocated. In addition, the adequacy of surveys in areas where ferrets have not been found has been supported through the observation of other infrequently observed small carnivores such as badgers, long-tailed weasels *(Mustela frenata)*, and bobcats *(Lynx rufus)* in those areas. In one instance, a long-tailed weasel (presumed to be a single individual) was observed in the

same location on successive nights by two separate crews, both without prior knowledge of its presence. On the other hand, ferrets were likely missed during surveys, as indicated by their detection during a subsequent survey. At least three consecutive nights of surveys were attempted in each area, but this was not always accomplished due to weather or other logistical constraints. Large areas of prairie dog habitat within the WCMA also required a tradeoff between survey effort intensity in a given area and adequate coverage of all suitable habitat. The recommendation of Biggins et al. (2006d) that an area should be covered at least every 30 to 60 minutes during that 3-day period was not met in WCMA surveys. Experience gained in the WCMA, as well as that reported by Biggins et al. (2006d) for another white-tailed prairie dog reintroduction site (Shirley Basin, Wyoming) and a Gunnison's prairie dog reintroduction site (Aubrey Valley, Arizona), indicates that a larger amount of effort is required for each ferret observation at these types of sites than at many black-tailed prairie dog reintroduction sites. This is probably due to the fact that white-tailed and Gunnison's prairie dog colonies are characterized by higher amounts of shrub cover and lower overall prairie dog densities, with concomitantly lower ferret densities. Given this information, managers should strive to meet or exceed the minimum survey requirements proposed by Biggins et al. (2006d) when dealing with ferret reintroductions at white-tailed and Gunnison's prairie dog reintroduction sites in order to gain reliable data on ferret survival and population size.

In the absence of plague outbreaks, and with no evidence to suggest that low levels of plague were reducing ferret survival, the most likely factor influencing ferret demographic rates in the WCMA was habitat quality (the density of prairie dogs and their burrows). Among current ferret reintroduction sites, the WCMA exhibits the lowest overall prairie dog density. Given that the most energetically expensive aspect of ferret natural history is the rearing of young by females, litter size might be predicted to decline in the absence of sufficient prey density. Variation in litter size is strongly tied to prey density for many species of carnivores (Fuller and Sievert 2001), and this relationship should theoretically be even more pronounced for a specialist predator such as the black-footed ferret where prey-switching is not a viable option. Biggins et al. (1993) predicted that a minimum prairie dog density of 3.63/ha is required to support a female ferret with young during the litter-rearing period, and many colonies within the WCMA met this minimum threshold. However, ferrets were not reencountered following release on most of these colonies and litters were only documented on colonies where prairie dog density was 5.5 prairie dogs/ha or higher.

Most of the recent research on black-footed ferrets has taken place at reintroduction sites within the range of black-tailed prairie dogs, a species that naturally occurs at higher densities than white-tailed prairie dogs (Hoogland 1981). Additional research on ferret resource selection and demography at white-tailed prairie dog sites is needed. Of the three ferret reintroductions attempted at white-tailed prairie dog sites, only one (Shirley Basin, Wyoming) currently supports a large population of ferrets that may be considered self-sustaining. However, the last known population of free-ranging ferrets from near Meeteetse, Wyoming, existed on a white-tailed prairie dog complex, evidence that white-tailed prairie dogs provide potentially high-quality habitat for ferrets. Much of the landscape within the range of the white-tailed prairie dog is still intact and in public ownership, providing good opportunities for the development of future release sites. Therefore, a better understanding of what conditions are needed to support a viable ferret population at white-tailed prairie dog sites will serve the greater conservation needs of ferrets.

APPENDIX A: COLONY-SPECIFIC PRAIRIE DOG TRANSECT SAMPLING

Summary for the Wolf Creek Management Area, 2004–2006

Table A-1. 2004 Wolf Creek Management Area transecting summary.

Colony	Size	Active Ratio	Ha Sampled	Active/Ha	Total/Ha	PD Density -Total	PD # Total	BFF Rating -Total	Ha Good	% Good	Active/Ha -Good	Total/Ha -Good	PD Density -Good	PD # Good	BFF Rating -Good
1	1281	0.65	12.600	16.51	41.98	2.43	3119	4.09	305.01	23.81	48.67	81.00	7.18	2189	2.87
2	86	0.90	1.125	16.89	35.56	2.49	214	0.00	22.94	26.67	63.33	80.00	9.34	214	0.00
3	52	0.56	0.945	9.52	26.46	1.40	73	0.00	0.00	0.00	0.00	0.00	0.00	0	0.00
4	36	0.09	0.600	3.33	40.00	0.49	18	0.00	0.00	0.00	0.00	0.00	0.00	0	0.00
5	25	0.00	0.300	0.00	23.33	0.00	0	0.00	0.00	0.00	0.00	0.00	0.00	0	0.00
6	170	2.50	1.935	33.59	47.03	4.95	842	1.10	73.80	43.41	61.90	76.79	9.13	674	0.88
7	44	0.00	0.525	0.00	17.14	0.00	0	0.00	0.00	0.00	0.00	0.00	0.00	0	0.00
8	473	0.87	8.295	35.08	75.35	5.17	2447	3.21	277.98	58.77	51.08	87.79	7.53	2094	2.74
9a	600	0.61	6.000	13.33	35.33	1.97	1180	1.55	90.00	15.00	37.78	57.78	5.57	501	0.66
9b	804	0.58	8.100	15.93	43.46	2.35	1889	2.48	208.48	25.93	41.90	71.43	6.18	1288	1.69
10	183	0.79	1.920	17.19	39.06	2.54	464	0.61	37.17	20.31	53.85	79.49	7.94	295	0.39
11	208	0.22	2.250	4.00	22.22	0.59	123	0.00	0.00	0.00	0.00	0.00	0.00	0	0.00
12	11	0.13	0.225	4.44	40.00	0.65	7	0.00	0.00	0.00	0.00	0.00	0.00	0	0.00
13	177	0.80	2.010	15.92	35.82	2.35	416	0.54	79.26	44.78	33.33	61.11	4.92	390	0.51
14	84	0.44	0.810	4.94	16.05	0.73	61	0.00	0.00	0.00	0.00	0.00	0.00	0	0.00
15	99	0.28	0.990	7.07	32.32	1.04	103	0.00	0.00	0.00	0.00	0.00	0.00	0	0.00
16	130	0.66	1.320	14.39	31.06	2.12	276	0.36	29.55	22.73	36.67	70.00	5.41	160	0.00
17	1460	0.80	9.750	13.85	31.08	2.04	2982	3.91	336.97	23.08	38.22	55.11	5.64	1899	2.49
18	323	0.83	3.398	20.31	44.73	3.00	967	1.27	180.40	55.85	31.09	46.90	4.58	827	1.08
19	17	0.00	0.300	0.00	10.00	0.00	0	0.00	0.00	0.00	0.00	0.00	0.00	0	0.00
20	372	0.76	3.750	31.20	72.00	4.60	1712	2.24	207.58	55.80	43.97	79.81	6.48	1346	1.76
23	361	1.13	3.750	28.53	53.87	4.21	1519	1.99	144.40	40.00	55.33	80.00	8.16	1178	1.54
24	312	0.82	1.800	27.78	61.67	4.10	1278	1.68	103.99	33.33	78.33	96.67	11.55	1201	1.57
25	397	0.93	2.400	22.08	45.83	3.26	1293	1.69	99.25	25.00	75.00	105.00	11.06	1098	1.44
26	22	3.00	0.300	40.00	53.33	5.90	130	0.00	22.00	100.00	40.00	53.33	5.90	130	0.00
30	24	0.00	0.300	0.00	26.67	0.00	0	0.00	0.00	0.00	0.00	0.00	0.00	0	0.00
34	14	0.00	0.188	0.00	10.64	0.00	0	0.00	0.00	0.00	0.00	0.00	0.00	0	0.00
Tot/Avg	7765		75.886			2.72	21113	26.72	2218.78	28.57			6.98	15484	19.62

Table A-2. 2005 Wolf Creek Management Area transecting summary.

Colony	Size	Active Ratio	Ha Sampled	Active/Ha	Total/Ha	PD Density -Total	PD # Total	BFF Rating -Total	Ha Good	% Good	Active/Ha -Good	Total/Ha -Good	PD Density -Good	PD # Good	BFF Rating -Good
1	1281	0.55	12.600	22.14	40.40	3.27	4183	5.48	457	35.71	46.44	65.56	6.85	3133	4.11
2	86	2.00	1.125	28.44	42.67	4.19	361	0.47	36	41.33	62.37	73.12	9.20	327	0.43
3	52	0.50	0.945	6.35	19.05	0.94	49	0.00	0	0.00	0.00	0.00	0.00	0	0.00
4	36	0.23	0.600	8.33	45.00	1.23	44	0.00	0	0.00	0.00	0.00	0.00	0	0.00
5	25	0.33	0.300	3.33	13.33	0.49	12	0.00	0	0.00	0.00	0.00	0.00	0	0.00
6	170	2.37	1.695	26.55	37.76	3.92	666	0.87	90	53.10	40.00	52.22	5.90	533	0.70
7	44	0.25	0.525	1.90	9.52	0.28	12	0.00	0	0.00	0.00	0.00	0.00	0	0.00
8	473	1.85	8.183	47.17	72.71	6.96	3290	4.31	386	81.67	53.42	80.51	7.88	3043	3.99
9a	600	0.83	6.000	18.67	41.17	2.75	1652	2.17	198	33.00	38.89	53.54	5.74	1136	1.49
9b	804	2.03	8.100	34.81	51.98	5.13	4127	5.41	462	57.41	53.55	69.03	7.90	3645	4.78
10	183	1.45	1.920	25.00	42.19	3.69	675	0.88	129	70.31	31.11	51.11	4.59	590	0.77
11	208	1.84	2.400	14.58	22.50	2.15	447	0.59	65	31.25	33.33	36.00	4.92	319	0.42
12	11	0.00	0.225	0.00	26.67	0.00	0	0.00	0	0.00	0.00	0.00	0.00	0	0.00
13	177	1.44	2.010	17.91	30.35	2.64	468	0.61	86	48.51	34.87	48.21	5.14	442	0.58
14	84	1.00	0.900	20.00	40.00	2.95	248	0.00	18	21.67	30.77	41.03	4.54	83	0.00
15	99	1.70	0.990	34.34	54.55	5.06	501	0.66	60	60.61	46.67	65.00	6.88	413	0.54
16	130	4.63	1.320	28.03	34.09	4.13	537	0.70	89	68.18	36.67	43.33	5.41	479	0.63
17	1460	2.50	9.750	26.46	37.03	3.90	5697	7.47	741	50.77	40.40	47.47	5.96	4416	5.79
18	323	9.13	3.398	42.97	47.68	6.34	2047	2.68	202	62.47	60.31	66.90	8.89	1795	2.35
19	17	0.00	0.300	0.00	16.67	0.00	0	0.00	0	0.00	0.00	0.00	0.00	0	0.00
20	372	3.52	3.750	52.53	67.47	7.75	2882	3.78	346	93.00	55.63	71.11	8.20	2838	3.72
23	361	2.81	3.600	37.50	50.83	5.53	1996	2.62	256	70.83	47.06	60.39	6.94	1775	2.33
24	312	1.08	1.800	31.67	61.11	4.67	1457	1.91	156	50.00	60.00	85.56	8.85	1380	1.81
25	397	3.00	2.400	30.00	40.00	4.42	1756	2.30	99	25.00	86.67	100.00	12.78	1269	1.66
26	22	3.00	0.165	36.36	48.48	5.36	118	0.00	22	100.00	36.36	48.48	5.36	118	0.00
30	24	3.50	0.300	23.33	30.00	3.44	83	0.00	0	0.00	0.00	0.00	0.00	0	0.00
34	14	0.00	0.188	0.00	21.28	0.00	83	0.00	0	0.00	0.00	0.00	0.00	0	0.00
Tot/Avg	7765		75.489			4.29	33308	42.91	3898	50.19			6.92	27734	36.10

Table A-3. 2006 Wolf Creek Management Area transecting summary.

Colony	Size	Active Ratio	Ha Sampled	Active/Ha	Total/Ha	PD Density - Total	PD # Total	BFF Rating -Total	Ha Good	% Good	Active/Ha - Good	Total/Ha - Good	PD Density - Good	PD # Good	BFF Rating - Good
1	1281	9.41	12.600	44.05	48.73	6.50	8322	10.91	854	66.67	61.19	67.26	9.02	7707	10.10
2	86	8.83	0.743	71.33	79.41	10.52	905	1.19	69	80.81	88.33	88.33	13.03	905	1.19
3	52	27.00	0.945	28.57	28.57	4.21	219	0.00	27	51.58	55.38	55.38	8.17	219	0.00
4	36	2.71	0.600	31.67	43.33	4.67	168	0.00	18	50.00	63.33	66.67	9.34	168	0.00
5	25	4.00	0.300	26.67	33.33	3.93	98	0.00	17	66.67	42.67	42.67	6.29	105	0.00
6	170	20.67	1.935	64.08	67.18	9.45	1607	2.11	144	84.50	71.56	75.23	10.55	1516	1.99
7	44	14.00	0.525	26.67	26.67	3.93	173	0.00	25	57.14	40.00	40.00	5.90	148	0.00
8	473	23.47	4.793	73.44	76.57	10.83	5123	6.71	455	96.09	76.22	78.83	11.24	5109	6.70
9a	600	8.72	6.000	52.33	58.33	7.72	4630	6.07	499	83.13	62.56	68.97	9.23	4602	6.03
9b	804	6.69	8.100	45.43	52.22	6.70	5387	7.06	610	75.93	55.45	62.11	8.18	4992	6.54
10	183	82.00	1.890	43.39	43.39	6.40	1171	1.53	139	76.20	52.78	52.78	7.78	1085	1.42
11	208	8.75	2.250	31.11	34.67	4.59	954	1.25	111	53.33	48.33	52.50	7.13	791	1.04
13	177	15.00	2.010	29.85	31.84	4.40	779	1.02	106	59.70	45.83	47.50	6.76	714	0.94
17	1460	14.22	9.450	40.63	43.49	5.99	8748	11.47	1043	71.43	51.41	53.78	7.58	7907	10.36
18	323	16.38	3.398	38.55	40.91	5.69	1836	2.41	212	65.56	52.53	54.32	7.75	1640	2.15
20	372	7.41	3.750	63.20	71.73	9.32	3467	4.54	365	98.00	64.22	72.93	9.47	3453	4.53
23	361	7.09	3.600	65.00	74.17	9.59	3460	4.54	331	91.67	69.70	78.79	10.28	3402	4.46
24	312	6.06	1.800	53.89	62.78	7.95	2480	3.25	260	83.33	61.33	71.33	9.04	2352	3.08
25	397	18.67	2.100	53.33	56.19	7.86	3122	4.09	170	42.86	107.78	111.11	15.89	2705	3.54
Tot/Avg	7364		66.789			7.15	52649	68.15	5455	74.06			9.08	49520	64.07

* Towns 12, 14, 15, 16, 19, 21, 26, 30, and 31 were not transected in 2006. These colonies total 401 hectares, or 5% of the prairie dog acreage in Wolf Creek.

APPENDIX B: SUMMARY OF BLACK-FOOTED FERRET RELEASE DATA

From the Wolf Creek Management Area, 2001–2006

Key to black-footed ferret origin and precondition site facilities:

BP	Browns Park, Colorado
CMZ	Cheyenne Mountain Zoo, Colorado
CRC	National Zoo Conservation and Research Center, Virginia
FCC	National Black-footed Ferret Conservation Center, Wyoming/Colorado
LZG	Louisville Zoological Garden, Kentucky
PHZ	Phoenix Zoo, Arizona
SD-WB	Conata Basin, South Dakota (wild-born)
TESF	Turner Endangered Species Fund, New Mexico
TOR	Toronto Zoo, Ontario, Canada

*All release locations are taken in the North American Datum of 1927.

Table B-1. 2001 Wolf Creek black-footed ferret release data.

Studbook #	Sex	Age	Head Chip	Rear Chip	Origin	Precondition Site	Release Date	Release Location (UTM)		
								Zone	Easting	Northing
2150	F	A	116*249*391	039*077*028	FCC	BP	11/15/01	12	-	-
2399	F	A	029*112*079	042*826*615	FCC	BP	11/15/01	12	-	-
2427	F	A	028*627*041	042*819*585	LZG	BP	11/15/01	12	-	-
2453	F	A	028*848*855	029*112*603	FCC	BP	11/15/01	12	-	-
2474	F	A	029*115*568	042*780*600	LZG	BP	11/15/01	12	-	-
2560	F	A	029*054*813	042*317*846	FCC	BP	11/15/01	12	-	-
2600	F	A	029*116*304	043*115*604	LZG	BP	11/15/01	12	-	-
3474	M	K	042*783*837	043*317*846	FCC	BP	11/15/01	12	-	-
3518	M	K	048*817*095	048*547*770	FCC	FCC	11/15/01	12	-	-
3519	M	K	048*562*603	048*380*781	FCC	FCC	11/15/01	12	-	-
3525	M	K	048*558*109	048*568*354	FCC	FCC	11/15/01	12	-	-
3541	M	K	048*535*081	048*794*876	FCC	FCC	11/23/01	12	-	-
3546	F	K	042*768*783	049*061*569	FCC	FCC	11/15/01	12	-	-
3553	M	K	048*524*850	048*559*611	FCC	FCC	11/15/01	12	-	-
3554	F	K	048*581*028	048*570*005	FCC	FCC	11/15/01	12	-	-
3560	M	K	048*552*357	048*585*081	FCC	FCC	11/15/01	12	-	-
3561	M	K	048*773*293	048*770*346	FCC	FCC	11/23/01	12	-	-
3566	F	K	048*580*616	048*784*083	FCC	FCC	11/15/01	12	-	-
3658	M	K	040*617*852	042*798*604	CMZ	BP	11/15/01	12	-	-
3659	M	K	039*080*034	039*124*575	CMZ	BP	11/15/01	12	-	-
3660	M	K	042*846*895	043*272*052	CMZ	BP	11/15/01	12	-	-
3675	M	K	042*793*859	043*315*367	LZG	BP	11/15/01	12	-	-
3677	M	K	042*810*315	042*817*792	LZG	BP	11/15/01	12	-	-
3684	M	K	043*301*017	042*843*623	LZG	BP	11/23/01	12	-	-
3685	F	K	042*825*332	040*616*546	LZG	BP	11/23/01	12	-	-
3686	F	K	040*605*533	042*872*322	LZG	BP	11/15/01	12	-	-
3690	M	K	043*110*572	043*315*851	LZG	FCC	11/15/01	12	-	-
3693	F	K	042*842*263	042*848*035	LZG	FCC	11/23/01	12	-	-
P245	F	K	040*583*571	040*583*533	BP	BP	11/23/01	12	-	-
P246	M	K	040*597*513	040*586*566	BP	BP	11/15/01	12	-	-
P252	M	K	040*581*340	040*530*351	BP	BP	11/23/01	12	-	-
P254	F	K	040*523*084	040*583*342	BP	BP	11/15/01	12	-	-
P255	M	K	030*821*121	031*001*023	BP	FCC	11/15/01	12	-	-
P256	F	K	031*056*811	030*827*588	BP	BP	11/15/01	12	-	-
P258	F	K	030*843*843	030*851*341	BP	BP	11/15/01	12	-	-

Table B-2. 2002 Wolf Creek black-footed ferret release data.

Studbook #	Sex	Age	Head Chip	Rear Chip	Origin	Precondition Site	Release Date	Zone	Easting	Northing
2334	F	A	029*110*564	043*121*296	LZG	BP	8/15/02	12	711339	467376
2346	F	A	114*549*493	049*057*569	FCC	FCC	11/19/02	12	703346	455674
2552	F	A	042*838*809	029*078*032	TOR	BP	11/7/02	12	703369	455732
2651	F	A	029*025*092	122*155*183	TOR	BP	10/17/02	12	716748	462985
2958	F	A	032*626*032	122*559*263	TOR	BP	10/17/02	12	709851	461387
3000	M	A	032*614*841	032*627*548	PHZ	BP	8/22/02	12	711463	467097
3039	F	A	032*624*852	032*620*074	PHZ	BP	8/22/02	12	711463	467097
3060	F	A	032*619*301	048*542*537	CRC	FCC	8/22/02	12	711165	467561
3715	M	K	042*880*124	048*794*845	TOR	FCC	8/15/02	12	711192	467557
3716	F	K	043*261*848	048*552*893	TOR	FCC	8/15/02	12	711117	467962
3770	M	K	056*847*323	057*081*017	FCC	FCC	11/7/02	12	703684	456008
3771	M	K	057*368*614	057*545*625	FCC	FCC	11/7/02	12	703552	455971
3772	M	K	057*549*037	057*276*884	FCC	FCC	11/7/02	12	703471	455788
3773	M	K	057*374*866	057*345*380	FCC	FCC	11/7/02	12	703583	456183
3774	F	K	057*046*096	057*356*629	FCC	FCC	11/7/02	12	703454	456085
3775	F	K	057*052*296	057*578*834	FCC	FCC	11/7/02	12	703317	455964
3776	M	K	056*858*812	056*879*056	FCC	FCC	11/7/02	12	703306	455591
P280	M	K	055*607*887	056*627*830	BP	BP	10/17/02	12	710106	461358
P281	M	K	056*638*293	055*627*770	BP	BP	10/17/02	12	716398	464252
P284	F	K	056*831*891	056*327*061	BP	BP	10/17/02	12	716523	463456
P285	F	K	056*772*366	055*827*771	BP	BP	10/17/02	12	716905	464376
P288	F	K	055*831*601	055*828*270	BP	BP	10/17/02	12	717757	462541
P303	F	K	055*616*099	056*095*348	BP	BP	10/17/02	12	717547	462516
P305	F	K	057*033*868	057*282*323	BP	BP	10/17/02	12	716668	463282
P315	M	K	040*526*064	057*001*373	BP	BP	10/17/02	12	717519	461988
P316	F	K	057*315*639	057*051*260	BP	BP	10/17/02	12	716902	462752
P317	F	K	056*874*790	057*044*879	BP	BP	10/17/02	12	717546	461867
P325	F	K	056*851*551	056*890*627	BP	BP	11/19/02	12	704013	457486

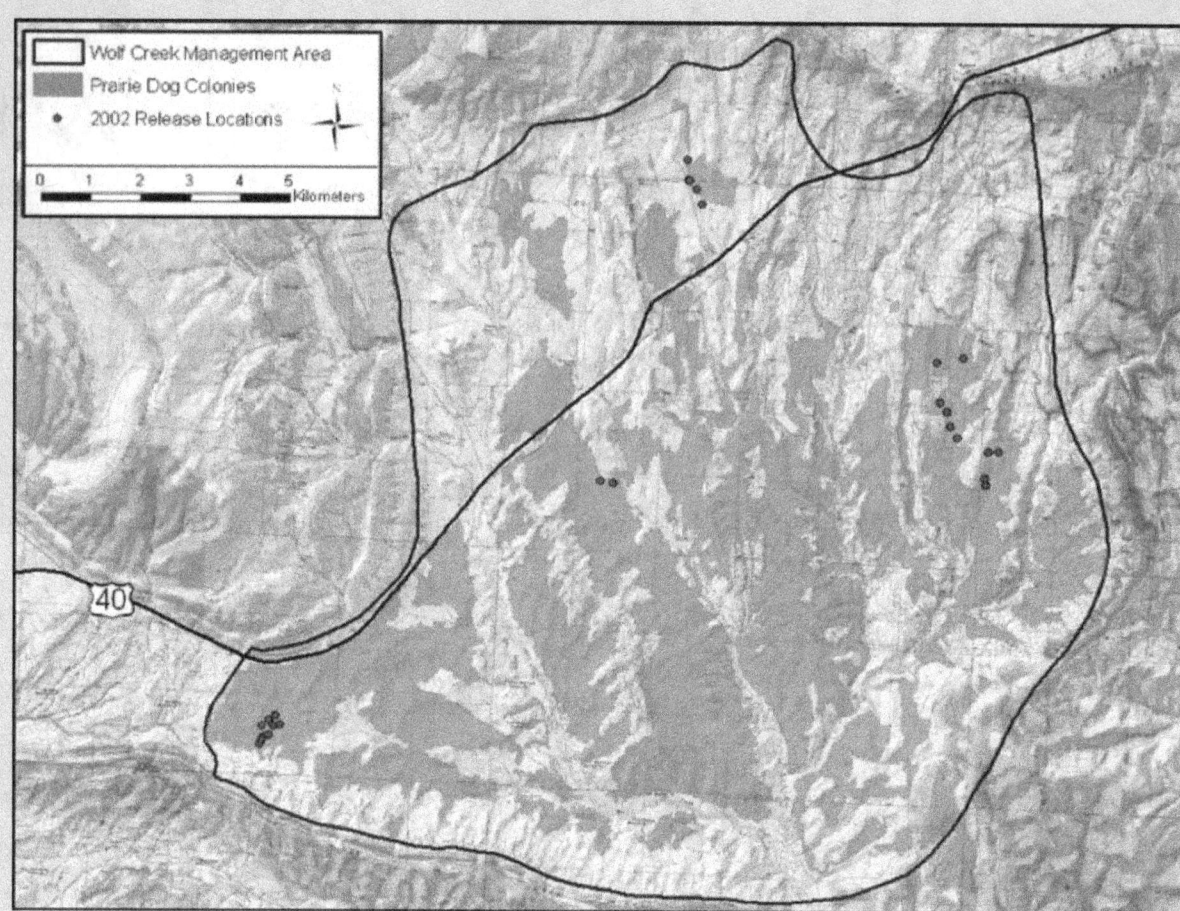

Figure B-1. Black-footed ferret release locations within the Wolf Creek Management Area — 2002.

Table B-3. 2003 Wolf Creek black-footed ferret release data.

Studbook #	Sex	Age	Head Chip	Rear Chip	Origin	Precondition Site	Release Date	Zone	Release Location (UTM) Easting	Northing
03-051	F	K	046*011*600	046*029*313	SD	SD-WB	10/10/03	12	716529	464441
03-056	M	K	046*113*280	046*326*030	SD	SD-WB	10/10/03	12	716634	4462579
03-062	F	K	046*372*000	046*017*360	SD	SD-WB	10/10/03	12	716958	462387
03-079	M	K	046*893*845	046*286*578	SD	SD-WB	10/10/03	12	716478	462620
03-093	F	K	046*264*867	046*295*857	SD	SD-WB	10/10/03	12	717437	464407
03-094	M	K	046*295*280	046*295*290	SD	SD-WB	10/10/03	12	716998	462565
03-103	M	K	046*076*521	046*391*338	SD	SD-WB	10/10/03	12	716774	462695
03-113	M	K	054*539*301	055*282*297	SD	SD-WB	10/10/03	12	716776	463024
03-134	M	K	055*058*118	054*033*871	SD	SD-WB	10/10/03	12	716985	464368
03-135	F	K	054*020*845	054*534*328	SD	SD-WB	10/10/03	12	716743	462880
3175	F	A	056*857*336	048*790*621	FCC	TESF	9/16/03	12	708665	456650
3198	F	A	027*521*288	057*276*058	FCC	BP	8/16/03	12	711731	462630
3199	F	A	027*370*011	057*270*345	FCC	BP	8/16/03	12	708641	465912
3204	F	A	040*524*580	056*869*637	FCC	BP	8/16/03	12	716405	464403
3236	F	A	039*080*086	057*551*782	FCC	BP	8/16/03	12	716108	464716
3259	M	A	049*073*328	010*353*824	TDR	TESF	9/16/03	12	705848	455059
3271	F	A	010*287*099	010*575*637	TDR	TESF	9/16/03	12	707305	459159
3272	F	A	011*070*258	011*047*016	BP	BP	10/14/03	12	713693	464207
3276	F	A	039*069*101	039*068*013	TDR	BP	8/16/03	12	716176	462725
3279	F	A	039*098*556	039*074*361	TDR	BP	10/14/03	12	711703	461187
3285	F	A	039*104*800	039*256*344	TDR	BP	8/16/03	12	708791	465308
3298	M	A	039*101*292	056*868*376	PHZ	TESF	9/16/03	12	706748	456050
3301	F	A	039*064*825	057*373*100	PHZ	TESF	9/16/03	12	707539	455136
3471	F	A	041*012*527	042*791*874	FCC	BP	10/14/03	12	715611	461952
3610	F	A	042*870*771	041*009*532	CRC	BP	9/24/03	12	711261	467622
3687	F	A	042*839*337	043*311*603	LZG	BP	10/30/03	12	-	
3981	M	K	047*265*372	057*540*550	PHZ	TESF	9/16/03	12	707015	457501
3983	F	K	047*514*059	056*855*276	PHZ	TESF	9/16/03	12	706992	455002
3987	F	K	047*370*779	057*052*882	PHZ	TESF	9/16/03	12	706520	458752
3989	F	K	047*342*602	057*003*848	PHZ	TESF	9/16/03	12	706722	457368
3990	M	K	048*532*788	057*342*283	PHZ	TESF	9/16/03	12	708720	455314
3992	F	K	056*888*543	057*058*256	PHZ	TESF	9/16/03	12	706239	455168
3993	F	K	057*522*117	056*894*059	PHZ	TESF	9/16/03	12	704992	454856
3994	M	K	042*771*857	042*805*043	CRC	CRC	9/16/03	12	707257	445342

Table B-3. 2003 Wolf Creek black-footed ferret release data (continued).

Studbook #	Sex	Age	Head Chip	Rear Chip	Origin	Precondition Site	Release Date	Zone	Easting	Northing
3995	M	K	043*105*564	042*856*105	CRC	CRC	9/16/03	12	706634	4456293
3996	M	K	042*797*010	043*314*895	CRC	CRC	9/16/03	12	707371	4458877
3997	F	K	042*846*636	043*115*276	CRC	CRC	9/16/03	12	707248	4457409
3998	F	K	043*289*042	057*585*598	CRC	CRC	9/16/03	12	706530	4456156
3999	F	K	042*789*857	042*833*803	CRC	CRC	9/16/03	12	706789	4456176
4000	M	K	057*351*526	056*847*349	FCC	FCC	9/16/03	12	706928	4459394
4001	M	K	057*364*784	056*856*260	FCC	FCC	9/16/03	12	706901	4459085
4002	F	K	057*266*553	057*257*123	FCC	FCC	9/16/03	12	706550	4455948
P385	F	K	040*531*789	040*550*548	BP	BP	9/24/03	12	713736	4464228
P386	F	K	040*604*045	040*538*341	BP	BP	9/24/03	12	711675	4461640
P387	M	K	040*526*592	057*057*059	BP	BP	10/14/03	12	711893	4460579
P388	M	K	040*601*061	040*553*882	BP	BP	10/14/03	12	715537	4461804
P389	F	K	040*348*021	040*615*341	BP	BP	10/14/03	12	708592	4465642
P390	F	K	040*613*376	040*588*801	TOR	BP	10/14/03	12	711321	4467802
P391	M	K	040*594*608	040*539*355	BP	BP	10/14/03	12	710731	4466738
P392	M	K	040*343*555	040*589*866	BP	BP	10/14/03	12	715705	4461389
P393	M	K	040*589*080	040*614*281	BP	BP	10/14/03	12	708181	4465824
P394	M	K	040*604*884	040*542*575	BP	BP	10/14/03	12	713815	4464543
P395	F	K	040*591*880	040*604*053	BP	BP	10/14/03	12	715612	4462120
P396	F	K	040*583*325	040*580*553	BP	BP	10/14/03	12	710744	4466589
P397	F	K	040*535*347	040*580*561	BP	BP	10/14/03	12	708645	4465986
P399	M	K	040*529*831	040*597*047	BP	BP	10/14/03	12	715769	4461389
P400	M	K	040*597*067	040*615*871	BP	BP	10/14/03	12	713815	4464543
P401	F	K	040*614*863	040*535*321	BP	BP	10/14/03	12	-	-
P402	F	K	040*609*782	040*608*855	BP	BP	10/14/03	12	711729	4461981
P404	M	K	040*528*870	040*564*871	BP	BP	10/30/03	12	706726	4456129
P405	M	K	040*546*281	040*600*371	BP	BP	11/19/03	12	704996	4454897
P406	F	K	040*595*116	040*559*357	BP	BP	10/30/03	12	706743	4458890
P407	F	K	040*618*545	040*604*569	BP	BP	10/30/03	12	706850	4456269

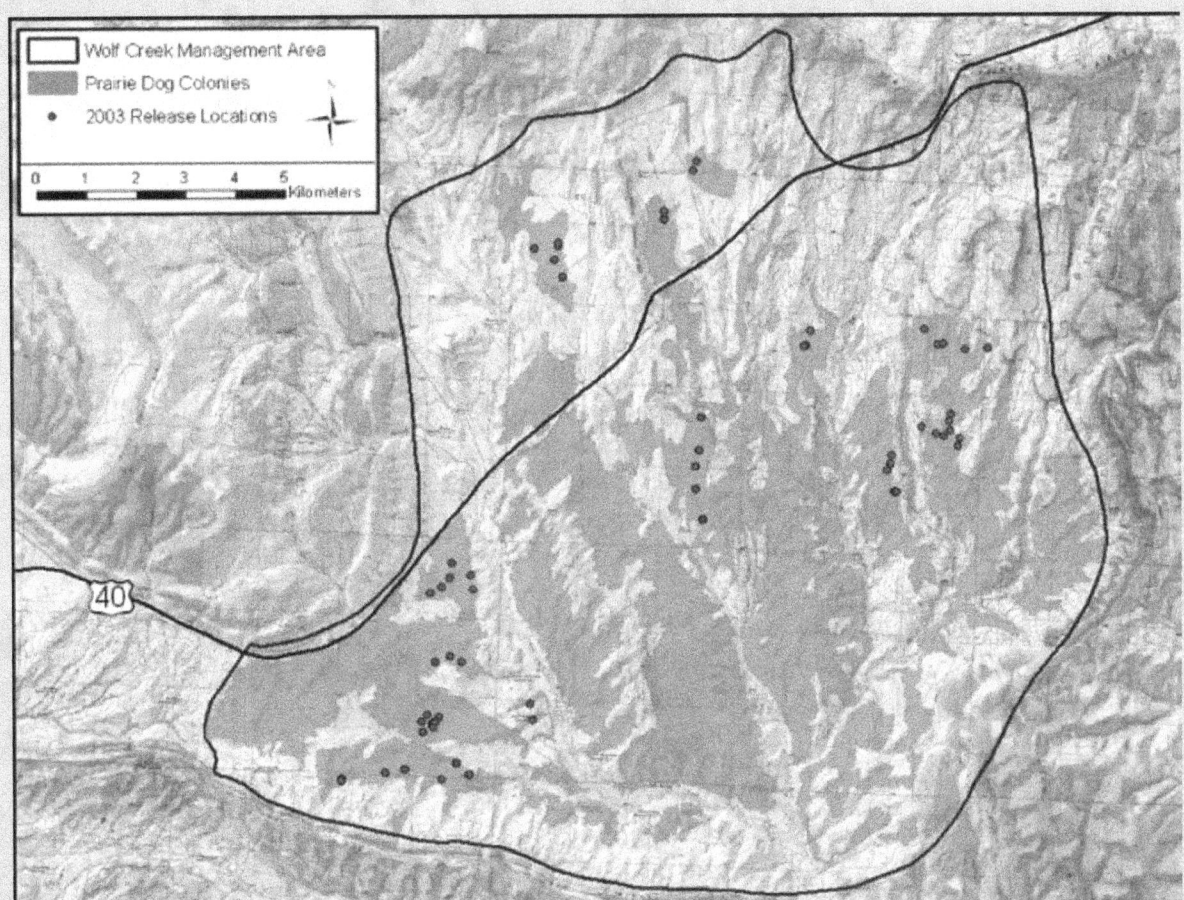

Figure B-2. Black-footed ferret release locations within the Wolf Creek Management Area — 2003.

Table B-4. 2004 Wolf Creek black-footed ferret release data.

Studbook #	Sex	Age	Head Chip	Rear Chip	Origin	Precondition Site	Release Date	Release Location (UTM)		
								Zone	Easting	Northing
3499	F	A	042*836*037	069*359*314	FCC	BP	10/6/04	12	717442	446856
4383	M	K	069*053*849	070*001*068	FCC	BP	10/6/04	12	717326	460820
4384	M	K	068*882*049	069*336*614	FCC	BP	10/6/04	12	715569	461859
4385	M	K	069*034*605	069*083*872	FCC	BP	10/6/04	12	708830	458342
4386	F	K	069*532*027	069*559*288	FCC	BP	10/6/04	12	706895	457687
4387	F	K	069*598*053	069*050*541	FCC	BP	10/6/04	12	711621	458190
4389	M	K	069*084*627	069*336*379	FCC	BP	10/6/04	12	716413	462097
4390	M	K	069*369*593	069*343*578	FCC	BP	10/6/04	12	711378	458135
4391	F	K	040*527*880	069*035*604	FCC	BP	10/6/04	12	716670	462147
4392	F	K	069*035*872	069*342*631	FCC	BP	10/6/04	12	707276	454937
4393	F	K	069*829*093	069*354*125	FCC	BP	10/6/04	12	709726	457672
4394	M	K	069*054*866	068*824*623	FCC	BP	10/6/04	12	711823	462771
4395	M	K	070*111*582	068*883*111	FCC	BP	10/6/04	12	709651	457627
4397	F	K	070*030*020	069*038*104	FCC	BP	10/6/04	12	711974	455263
4400	M	K	069*331*842	069*053*599	FCC	BP	10/6/04	12	709601	457986
4404	M	K	069*338*602	069*057*623	FCC	BP	10/6/04	12	710206	455022
4405	M	K	068*830*316	069*034*860	FCC	BP	10/6/04	12	707139	455014
4406	M	K	069*041*620	069*032*887	FCC	BP	10/6/04	12	711711	458257
4410	M	K	069*340*520	069*363*011	FCC	BP	10/6/04	12	706796	457697
4411	F	K	068*893*114	069*105*027	FCC	FCC	10/22/04	12	715354	460753
4412	F	K	069*330*840	069*033*342	FCC	FCC	10/6/04	12	708865	458786
4413	F	K	069*081*840	068*886*579	FCC	BP	10/6/04	12	711723	455382
4414	F	K	069*256*854	068*842*326	FCC	BP	10/6/04	12	710500	456274
4445	M	K	069*807*553	077*100*803	FCC	FCC	10/22/04	12	710863	465471
4452	M	K	069*076*092	069*354*798	FCC	FCC	10/8/04	12	706492	455803
4457	F	K	068*830*561	068*828*804	FCC	FCC	10/8/04	12	711108	468891
4472	M	K	069*823*263	076*084*597	FCC	FCC	10/22/04	12	710044	461629
4481	M	K	070*020*817	069*065*628	FCC	FCC	10/8/04	12	706501	458754
4485	M	K	070*282*799	076*876*273	FCC	FCC	10/22/04	12	710688	465250
4495	M	K	065*867*512	077*095*007	FCC	FCC	10/22/04	12	710276	460707
4500	M	K	066*005*835	069*364*890	FCC	FCC	10/8/04	12	706715	459030
4501	M	K	070*296*272	069*074*024	FCC	FCC	10/8/04	12	711264	467588
4507	F	K	069*877*565	069*338*290	FCC	FCC	10/8/04	12	706719	458867
4523	F	K	066*346*061	076*884*834	FCC	FCC	10/22/04	12	708907	461258

Table B-4. 2004 Wolf Creek black-footed ferret release data (continued).

Studbook #	Sex	Age	Head Chip	Rear Chip	Origin	Precondition Site	Release Date	Release Location (UTM)		
								Zone	Easting	Northing
4539	F	K	066*347*337	068*042*088	FCC	FCC	10/8/04	12	711181	4467758
4634	F	K	076*836*052	069*272*095	FCC	FCC	11/16/04	12	711877	4460968
4636	M	K	077*104*058	069*336*329	FCC	FCC	11/16/04	12	709648	4461459
4671	M	K	077*007*062	069*267*070	FCC	FCC	11/16/04	12	711725	4462447
4680	M	K	077*111*335	069*529*314	FCC	FCC	11/16/04	12	711778	4461909
4736	M	K	077*087*836	069*792*583	FCC	FCC	11/16/04	12	706721	4458939
4739	M	K	076*783*575	068*829*861	FCC	FCC	11/16/04	12	709847	4461320
4741	F	K	076*818*586	069*025*283	FCC	FCC	11/16/04	12	706721	4458938
4745	F	K	077*120*290	068*843*557	FCC	FCC	11/16/04	12	709896	4461316
4757	F	K	077*059*273	069*351*273	FCC	FCC	11/16/04	12	711617	4462433

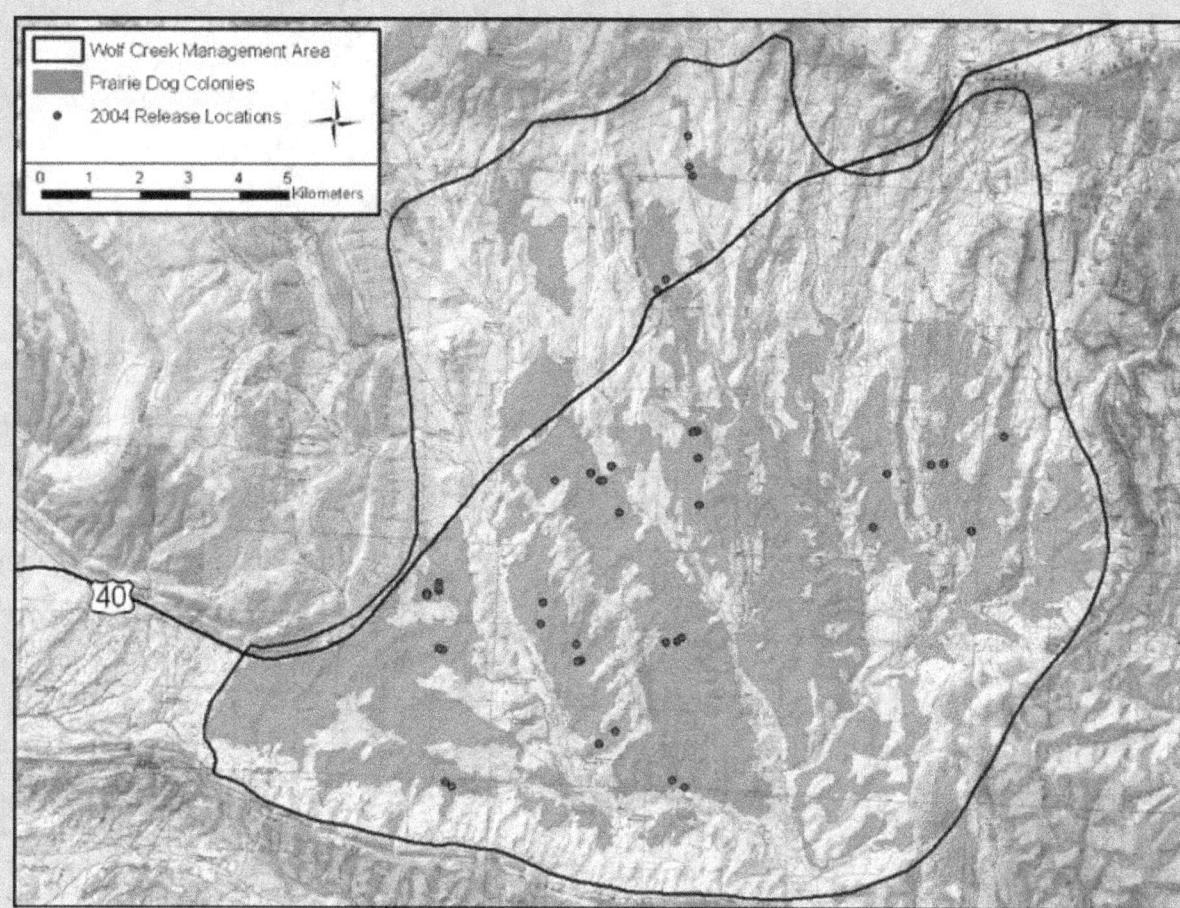

Figure B-3. Black-footed ferret release locations within the Wolf Creek Management Area – 2004.

Table B-5. 2005 Wolf Creek black-footed ferret release data.

Studbook #	Sex	Age	Head Chip	Rear Chip	Origin	Precondition Site	Release Date	Release Location (UTM)		
								Zone	Easting	Northing
4845	M	K	040*257*340	107*313*015	FCC	BP	10/13/05	12	716977	4464372
4847	M	K	041*381*541	107*265*515	FCC	BP	10/13/05	12	716925	4464537
4854	F	K	041*362*049	107*112*119	FCC	BP	10/13/05	12	716966	4464228
4855	M	K	041*326*561	107*258*008	FCC	BP	10/13/05	12	706851	4459353
4859	M	K	041*319*839	107*304*824	FCC	BP	10/13/05	12	707110	4459045
4868	M	K	041*361*849	107*298*033	FCC	BP	10/13/05	12	707417	4458927
4875	M	K	040*534*343	107*280*546	FCC	BP	10/19/05	12	717186	4459252
4883	F	K	041*335*582	107*265*632	FCC	BP	10/19/05	12	717843	4458881
4884	F	K	041*338*553	107*119*029	FCC	BP	10/19/05	12	717225	4459497
4895	M	K	040*595*306	107*306*071	FCC	BP	10/19/05	12	715333	4463891
4898	F	K	040*607*127	107*120*346	FCC	BP	10/19/05	12	715124	4463293
4899	M	K	040*580*263	107*127*383	FCC	BP	10/19/05	12	717546	4458830
4911	M	K	040*598*268	107*296*886	FCC	BP	10/19/05	12	714943	4463732
4934	F	K	041*517*828	107*270*354	FCC	BP	10/26/05	12	717398	4459655
4944	M	K	107*285*090	107*289*629	CMZ	BP	10/26/05	12	717586	4458853
4948	M	K	041*337*054	107*122*768	FCC	BP	10/26/05	12	717294	4466316
4951	F	K	041*291*001	107*273*307	FCC	BP	10/26/05	12	718219	4463357
4954	M	K	107*121*294	107*266*614	CMZ	BP	10/26/05	12	703222	4455511
4997	M	K	041*314*559	107*279*591	FCC	BP	11/2/05	12	703425	4455486

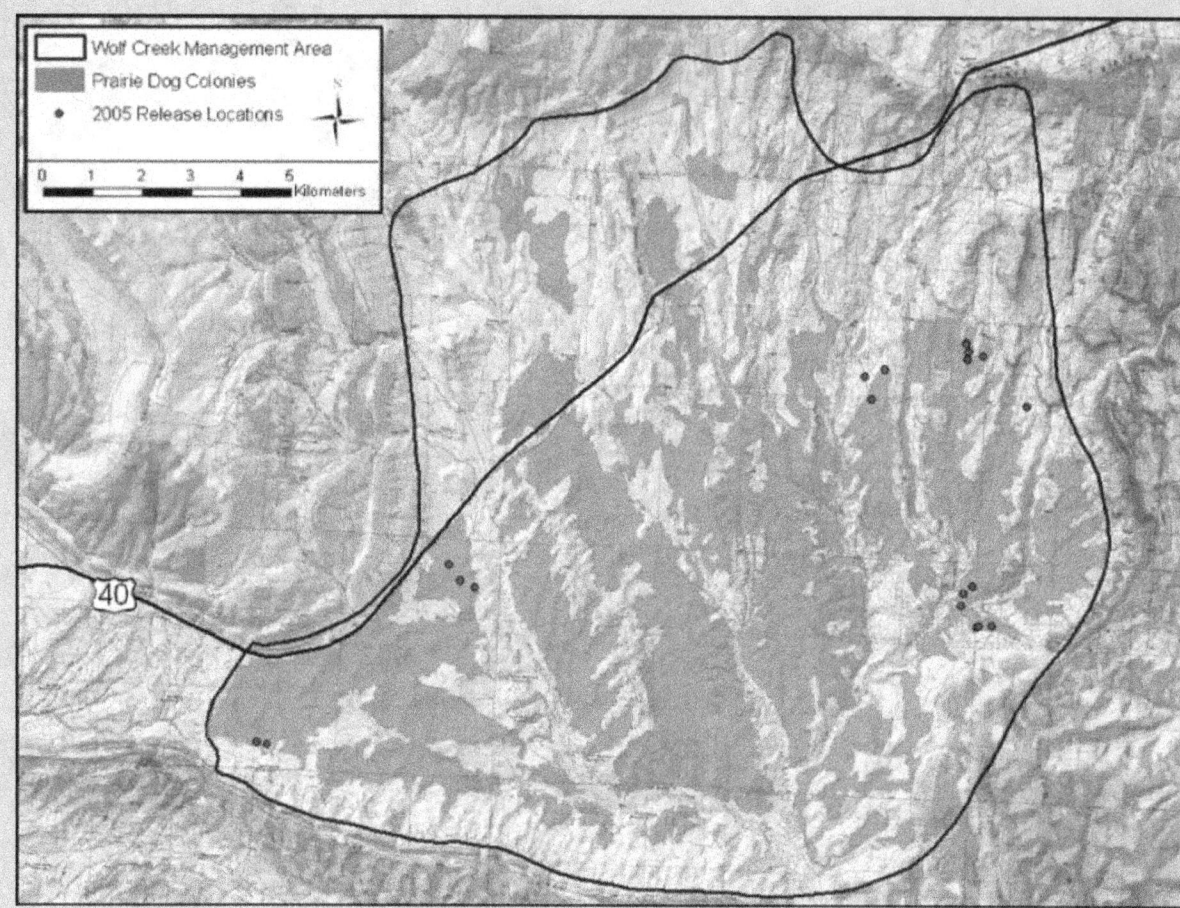

Figure B-4. Black-footed ferret release locations within the Wolf Creek Management Area — 2005.

Table B-6. 2006 Wolf Creek black-footed ferret release data.

Studbook #	Sex	Age	Head Chip	Rear Chip	Origin	Precondition Site	Release Date	Zone	Release Location (UTM)	
									Easting	Northing
4008	F	A	057*344*620	056*859*326	TOR	BP	9/26/06	12	713910	4456751
5123	M	K	081*377*294	081*377*531	LZG	BP	10/24/06	12	710258	4455840
5139	M	K	107*278*533	107*305*320	FCC	BP	9/26/06	12	716676	4458730
5144	M	K	107*122*628	107*112*307	FCC	BP	10/8/06	12	706733	4458864
5153	F	K	081*087*782	057*127*048	FCC	BP	9/26/06	12	717200	4459237
5167	M	K	073*621*841	056*870*616	FCC	BP	9/26/06	12	714079	4456265
5172	M	K	099*090*858	097*824*564	FCC	BP	9/26/06	12	715347	4457047
5177	F	K	074*055*114	107*293*043	FCC	BP	9/26/06	12	715137	4463301
5179	M	K	098*606*839	098*675*795	FCC	BP	9/26/06	12	715343	4463971
5207	M	K	042*788*062	081*378*831	LZG	BP	10/24/06	12	715385	4456744
5212	F	K	081*377*296	081*378*891	LZG	BP	10/24/06	12	703543	4453679
5219	M	K	098*789*065	099*092*588	FCC	BP	10/8/06	12	710578	4456429
5221	M	K	098*886*023	091*905*366	FCC	BP	10/8/06	12	703957	4450037
5235	F	K	102*581*009	081*377*006	CMZ	BP	10/24/06	12	716263	4462523
5237	M	K	098*026*117	098*363*872	FCC	BP	10/8/06	12	706444	4458713
5247	M	K	098*878*799	098*339*106	FCC	BP	10/8/06	12	703166	4455405
5248	F	K	098*090*066	098*637*592	FCC	BP	10/8/06	12	703209	4455506
5255	F	K	107*112*854	107*263*559	FCC	BP	10/24/06	12	716603	4462242
5300	M	K	107*110*376	081*377*280	LZG	BP	10/24/06	12	714285	4457188
5330	M	K	107*109*259	081*379*016	LZG	BP	10/24/06	12	718562	4459592
5340	M	K	098*001*259	081*377*519	LZG	BP	10/24/06	12	717422	4459812
5414	M	K	074*083*816	073*355*532	FCC	BP	10/24/06	12	716415	4462410
5425	M	K	074*084*316	073*837*891	FCC	BP	10/24/06	12	718356	4459512
5431	F	K	073*872*113	074*114*808	FCC	BP	11/7/06	12	709414	4457784
5436	F	K	073*328*074	074*266*024	FCC	BP	11/7/06	12	716971	4464748
5439	M	K	098*033*527	074*041*373	FCC	BP	11/7/06	12	709302	4457565
5441	F	K	073*633*845	073*310*845	FCC	BP	11/9/06	12	716395	4463404
5442	F	K	073*814*546	074*310*257	FCC	BP	11/7/06	12	716420	4464611

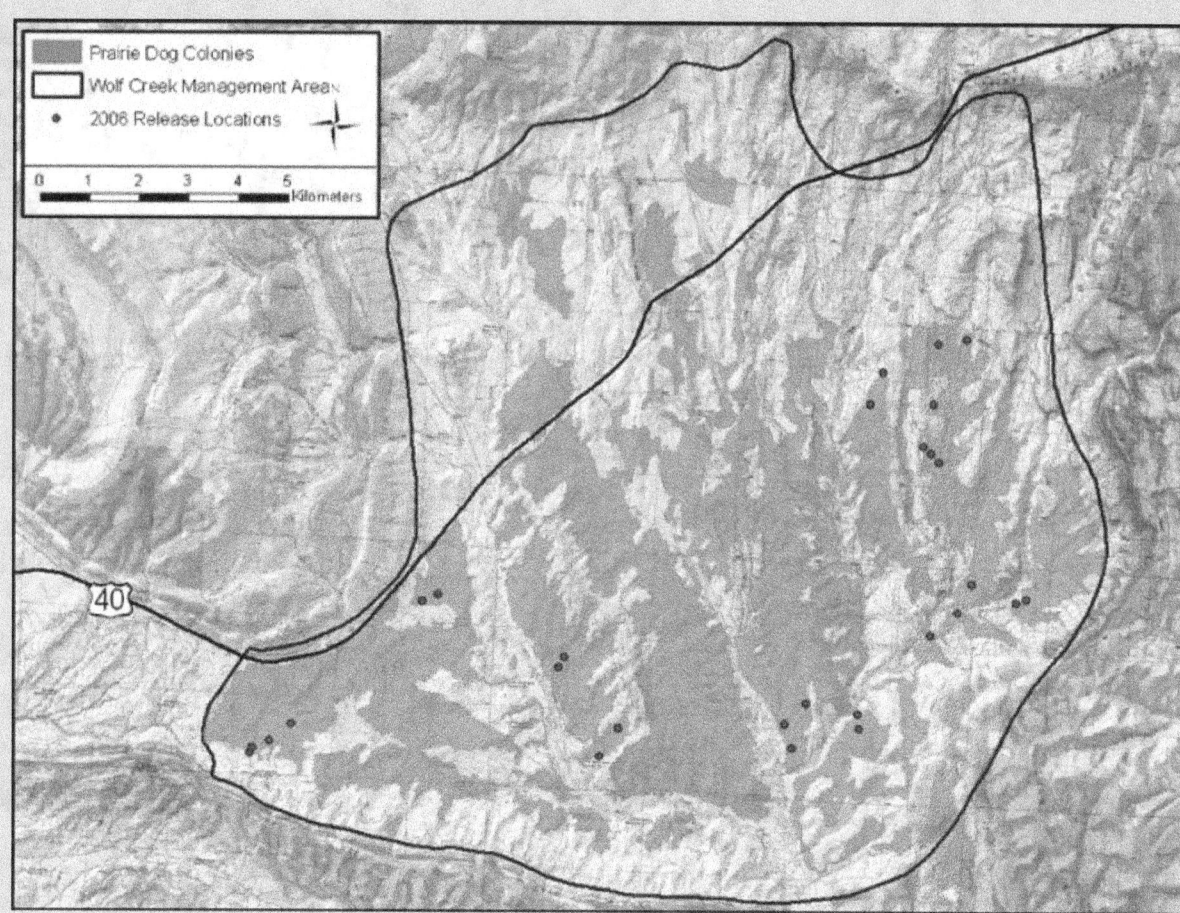

Figure B-5. Black-footed ferret release locations within the Wolf Creek Management Area – 2006.

LITERATURE CITED

Anderson, E., S.C. Forrest, T.W. Clark, and L. Richardson. 1986. Paleobiology, biogeography, and systematics of the black-footed ferret, *Mustela nigripes* (Audubon and Bachman), 1851. Great Basin Naturalist Memoirs 8:11-62.

Barnes, A.M. 1993. A review of plague and its relevance to prairie dog populations and the black-footed ferret. *In* J.L. Oldemeyer, D.E. Biggins, B.J. Miller, and R. Crete (editors). Management of prairie dog complexes for the reintroduction of the black-footed ferret. Biological Report 13, U.S. Fish and Wildlife Service, Washington, DC. p. 28-37.

Biggins, D.E, B.J. Miller, L.R. Hanebury, B. Oakleaf, A.H. Farmer, R. Crete, and A. Dood. 1993. A technique for evaluating black-footed ferret habitat. *In* J.L. Oldemeyer, D.E. Biggins, B.J. Miller, and R. Crete (editors). Management of prairie dog complexes for the reintroduction of the black-footed ferret. Biological Report 13, U.S. Fish and Wildlife Service, Washington, DC. p. 73-88.

Biggins, D.E., J.L. Godbey, L.R. Hanebury, B. Luce, P.E. Marinari, M.R. Matchett, and A. Vargas. 1998. The effect of rearing methods on survival of reintroduced black-footed ferrets. Journal of Wildlife Management 62:643-653.

Biggins, D.E., J.M. Lockhart, and J.L. Godbey. 2006a. Evaluating habitat for black-footed ferrets: revision of an existing model. *In* J.E. Roelle, B.J. Miller, J.L. Godbey, and D.E. Biggins (editors). Recovery of the black-footed ferret: progress and continuing challenges. U.S. Geological Survey Scientific Investigations Report 2005-5293. Reston, VA. p. 143-150.

Biggins, D.E., J.L. Godbey, M.R. Matchett, and T.M. Livieri. 2006b. Habitat preferences and intraspecific competition in black-footed ferrets. *In* J.E. Roelle, B.J. Miller, J.L. Godbey, and D.E. Biggins (editors). Recovery of the black-footed ferret: progress and continuing challenges. U.S. Geological Survey Scientific Investigations Report 2005-5293. Reston, VA. p. 129-140.

Biggins, D.E., J.L. Godbey, T.M. Livieri, M.R. Matchett, and B.D. Bibles. 2006c. Postrelease movements and survival of adult and young black-footed ferrets. *In* J.E. Roelle, B.J. Miller, J.L. Godbey, and D.E. Biggins (editors). Recovery of the black-footed ferret: progress and continuing challenges. U.S. Geological Survey Scientific Investigations Report 2005-5293. Reston, VA. p. 191-200.

Biggins, D.E., J.L. Godbey, M.R. Matchett, L.R. Hanebury, T.M. Livieri, and P.E. Marinari. 2006d. Monitoring black-footed ferrets during reestablishment of free-ranging populations: discussion of alternative methods and recommended minimum standards. *In* J.E. Roelle, B.J. Miller, J.L. Godbey, and D.E. Biggins (editors). Recovery of the black-footed ferret: progress and continuing challenges. U.S. Geological Survey Scientific Investigations Report 2005-5293. Reston, VA. p. 155-174.

Campbell, T.M., III, D. Biggins, S. Forrest, and T.W. Clark. 1985. Spotlighting as a method to locate and study black-footed ferrets. *In* S.H. Anderson and D.B. Inkley (editors). Black-footed ferret workshop proceedings, Laramie, Wyoming, September 18-19, 1984. Wyoming Game and Fish Department, Cheyenne. p. 24.1-24.7.

Clark, T.W., T.M. Campbell, M.H. Schroeder, and L. Richardson. 1984. Handbook of methods for locating black-footed ferrets. Wyoming BLM Wildlife Technical Bulletin No. 1. U.S. Bureau of Land Management, Cheyenne, Wyoming. 55pp.

Cully, J.F., Jr., and E.S. Williams. 2001. Interspecific comparisons of sylvatic plague in prairie dogs. Journal of Mammalogy 82:894-905.

Forrest, S.C., T.W. Clark, L. Richardson, and T.M. Campbell. 1985. Black-footed ferret habitat: some management and reintroduction considerations. Wyoming BLM Wildlife Technical Bulletin No. 2. U.S. Bureau of Land Management, Cheyenne, Wyoming. 49pp.

Forrest, S.C., D.E. Biggins, L. Richardson, T.W. Clark, T.M. Campbell, K.A. Fagerstone, and E.T. Thorne. 1988. Population attributes for the black-footed ferret *(Mustela nigripes)* at Meeteetse, Wyoming, 1981-1985. Journal of Mammalogy 69:261-273.

Fuller, T.K., and P.R. Sievert. 2001. Carnivore demography and the consequences of changes in prey availability. *In* J.L. Gittleman, S.M. Funk, D.W. Macdonald, and R.K. Wayne (editors). Carnivore conservation. Cambridge University Press, Cambridge, United Kingdom. p. 163-178.

Hillman, C.N. and T.W. Clark. 1980. *Mustela nigripes.* Mammalian Species 126:1-3.

Hoogland, J.L. 1981. The evolution of coloniality in white-tailed and black-tailed prairie dogs (Sciuridae: *Cynomys leucurus* and *C. ludovicianus*). Ecology 62:252-272.

Jachowski, D.S. 2007. Resource selection by black-footed ferrets in relation to the spatial distribution of prairie dogs. M.S. Thesis, University of Missouri, Columbia. 61pp.

Linder, R.L., R.B. Dahlgren, and C.N. Hillman. 1972. Black-footed ferret–prairie dog interrelationships. *In* Symposium on rare and endangered wildlife of the southwestern United States. New Mexico Department of Game and Fish, Santa Fe. p. 22-37.

Lockhart, J.M., E.T. Thorne, and D.R. Gober. 2006. A historical perspective on recovery of the black-footed ferret and the biological and political challenges affecting its future. *In* J.E. Roelle, B.J. Miller, J.L. Godbey, and D.E. Biggins (editors). Recovery of the black-footed ferret: progress and continuing challenges. U.S. Geological Survey Scientific Investigations Report 2005-5293. Reston, VA. p. 6-19.

Matchett, R. 1999. Black-footed ferret recovery activities on the UL Bend and Charles M. Russell National Wildlife Refuges, Phillips County, Montana. 1998 annual report and 5-year summary. U.S. Fish and Wildlife Service, Lewistown, Montana. 38pp.

Maxfield, B.D. Undated. Summary review of black-footed ferret reintroduction in Utah, 1999–2003. Wildlife Section, Mammals Program. Utah Division of Wildlife Resources, Salt Lake City. 22pp.

Richardson, L., T.W. Clark, S.C. Forrest, and T.M. Campbell. 1987. Winter ecology of black-footed ferrets *(Mustela nigripes)* at Meeteetse, Wyoming. The American Midland Naturalist 117:225-239.

U.S. Fish and Wildlife Service. 1988. Black-footed ferret recovery plan. U.S. Fish and Wildlife Service, Denver, Colorado. 154pp.

U.S. Fish and Wildlife Service. 1998. Endangered and threatened wildlife and plants: establishment of a nonessential experimental population of black-footed ferrets in northwestern Colorado and northeastern Utah. Final rule. Federal Register 63:52824-52841.

U.S. Fish and Wildlife Service, Bureau of Land Management, and Colorado Division of Wildlife. 1995. A cooperative management plan for black-footed ferrets, Little Snake Management Area, Colorado. 97pp.

Van Pelt, W.E. and R.A. Winstead. 2003. Review of black-footed ferret reintroduction in Arizona, 1996–2001. Nongame and Endangered Wildlife Program Technical Report 222. Arizona Game and Fish Department, Phoenix. 23pp.

Western Regional Climate Center. 2007. *http://www.wrcc.dri.edu/*. Accessed April 25, 2007.

Whitelaw, A., A. Hurt, L. Belmonte, and E. Hollowed. 2005. Black-footed ferret detection by detection dogs in the Wolf Creek reintroduction area, CO, May 2005. Working Dogs for Conservation, Bozeman, Montana. 12pp.

Williams, E.S., K. Mills, D.R. Kwiatkowski, E.T. Thorne, and A. Boerger-Fields. 1994. Plague in a black-footed ferret *(Mustela nigripes)*. Journal of Wildlife Diseases 30:581-585.

Williams, E.S., E.T. Thorne, M.J.G. Appel, and D.W. Belitsky. 1988. Canine distemper in black-footed ferrets *(Mustela nigripes)* from Wyoming. Journal of Wildlife Diseases 24:385-398.

Wolf Creek Work Group. 2001. A cooperative plan for black-footed ferret reintroduction and management—Wolf Creek and Coyote Basin Management Areas, Moffat and Rio Blanco Counties, Colorado. 64pp.

www.ingramcontent.com/pod-product-compliance
Lightning Source LLC
Chambersburg PA
CBHW052015280526
45793CB00005B/987